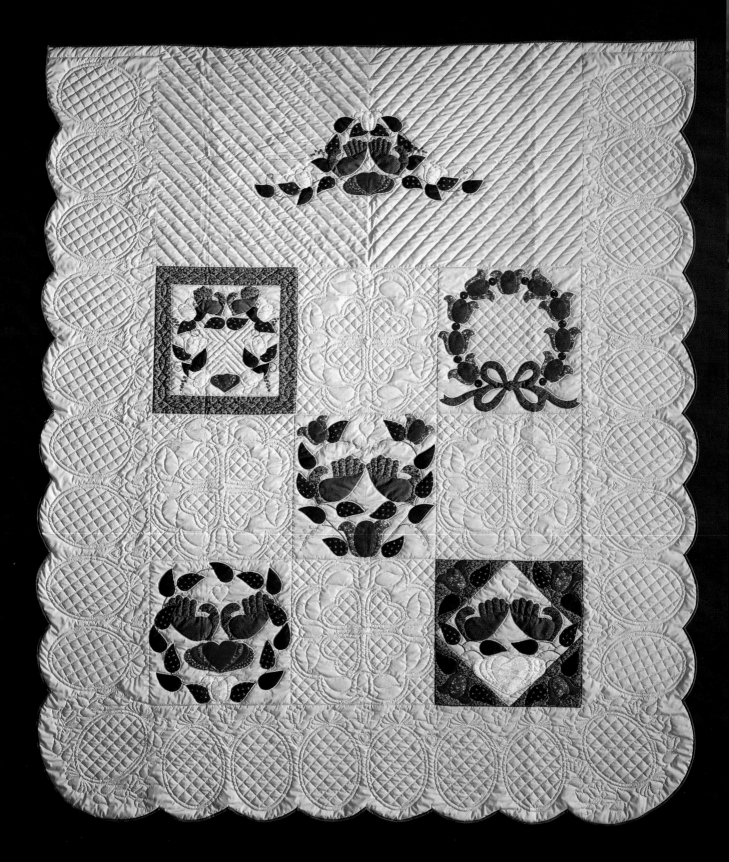

The Country Bride Quilt Collection

The
Country Bride
Quilt
Collection

Cheryl A. Benner
and
Rachel T. Pellman

Good Books
Intercourse, PA 17534

Acknowledgments

Design by Cheryl A. Benner
Cover and color photography by
Jonathan Charles
Author photo by Kenneth Pellman

The Country Bride Quilt *Collection*

©1991 by Good Books,
Intercourse, PA 17534
International Standard Book Number:
1-56148-015-0
Library of Congress Catalog Card Number:
91-70666

Library of Congress Cataloging-in-Publication Data

Benner, Cheryl A., 1962—
    The country bride quilt collection/Cheryl A. Benner
    and Rachel T. Pellman.

        p.   cm.
ISBN   1-56148-015-0   : $12.95

        1. Quilting—Patterns.   2. Patchwork—Patterns,
I. Pellman, Rachel T. (Rachel Thomas)   II. Title.
TT835.B334   1991   746.9′7—dc20   91-70666
                                                    CIP

Table of Contents

7   The Country Quilt Collection
8   How to Begin
9   Applique Quilts
9   Preparing Background fabric for
       Appliqueing
9   Making Templates
9   Appliqueing
10   Assembling the Appliqued Quilt Top
10   Quilting on Applique and Pieced Quilts
10   Marking Quilting Designs
11   Quilting
11   Binding
12   To Display Quilts
12   Other Projects
13   Signing and Dating Quilts
15   Cutting Layouts/Assembly Instructions
       for the Country Bridesmaid Quilt
16   Cutting Layouts/Assembly Instructions
       for the Country Romance Quilt
17   Cutting Layouts/Assembly Instructions
       for the Country Trousseau Quilt
18   Cutting Layouts/Assembly Instructions
       for the Country Wedding Wreath Quilt
19   Cutting Layouts/Assembly Instructions
       for the Country Courtship Quilt
21   Country Bride Collection Applique
       Templates
47   Country Bridesmaid Quilt Applique Layout
59   Country Trousseau Quilt Applique Layout
77   Country Bride Collection Alternate Patch
       Applique and Quilting Layout
95   Country Romance Quilt Applique Layout
103 Country Romance Quilt Sashing Template
105 Country Wedding Wreath Applique Layout
141 Country Bride Collection Pillow Throw
151 Country Courtship Quilt Applique Layout
165 Country Bride Collection Quilting Template
       for the Cameo Border
175 About the Old Country Store
176 About the Authors

The Country Bridesmaid

The Country Romance

The Country Trousseau

The Country Wedding Wreath

The Country Courtship

The Old Country Store staff created the original Country Bride quilt in 1983 in response to a request from *Bride's* magazine. The quilt appeared in the June issue of that magazine and since then has hung in The Old Country Store in Intercourse, Pennsylvania. We were delighted by the delicate beauty of the original quilt, but none of us was prepared for the exuberant reactions it elicited from the general public. Quilters who frequented our store brought friends to see this quilt and there was a great cry for the pattern. Non-quilters placed orders for a Country Bride quilt of their own, many of them requesting that it be "just like the original." In short, people have loved it.

After many years of Country Bride quilts, we have now created partner quilts which we present here as *The* Country Bride *Collection.* These patterns use the popular motifs from the original Country Bride, but arrange them in exciting new ways and add a few unusual twists.

The Country Bride is destined to be one of the most popular quilt designs of recent years. These new designs will only broaden its scope and provide new avenues for its enjoyment.

Here are five patterns. Additionally, we offer a Sampler quilt which combines the five designs on one quilt. Each quilt uses the same pillow throw and border quilting motifs.

The Country Bridesmaid

The Country Bridesmaid echoes the love theme in its applique designs. Five patches have paired lovebirds nestled within a heart of tulips, leaves and berries. The four alternate patches consist of appliqued hearts and tulips. When the nine patches are combined, the resulting quilt top is lush and full. Quilted cameos grace its border and a scalloped binding follows the lower edge of the quilting motifs.

The Country Romance

Nine identical patches separated with sashing combine to make the Country Romance quilt. Lovebirds perch at the top of a wreath of tulips. They face each other with their breasts touching, heads turned shyly away. The center of the applique design is filled with quilted chevron lines. The sashing is quilted with a leafy vine and the border with delicate cameo shapes.

The Country Trousseau

Five patches of this pattern are composed of a square and its surrounding triangles (of a differing fabric), held together visually by applique design. The alternate four patches combine appliqued hearts and tulips inside a quilted scallop. The entire top is surrounded by a border of quilted cameos.

The Country Bride Collection

The Country Wedding Wreath

This pattern uses five square patches, each tipped on an angle and squared off with the addition of triangles on four sides. The center patch uses birds, tulips and daisies. The four surrounding patches hold a tulip wreath secured with a graceful bow. Each triangle echoes the daisy and tulip theme from the center patch. Cross-hatch filled cameos fill the generously quilted border.

The Country Courtship

Lovebirds atop a heart fan are confined within an airy leaf vine in the Country Courtship pattern. The applique patches alternate with blocks pieced in an Around the World design. The pieced patches are quilted in straight lines; applique patches are outline quilted. The border uses the quilted cameo motif.

The Country Bride Collection Sampler

If the limitations of one pattern seem confining, a sampler quilt provides a pleasant alternative. Here, each of the five designs is executed on its own patch; each is placed against a quilted version of the alternate applique design of hearts and tulips. Cameo quilting motifs fill the border and a scalloped edge finishes the quilt.

Any of these designs is adaptable for pillows and/or wall hangings. A single patch makes a lovely pillow. A single patch with the addition of a border translates to a beautiful wall hanging.

We present *The* Country Bride *Collection* for your enjoyment. Its possibilities are as numerous and varied as the quilters who make them. Happy quilting!

How to Begin

Read the following instructions thoroughly before beginning work on your quilt.

Wash all fabrics before cutting them. This process will both preshrink and test them for colorfastness. If the fabric is not colorfast after one washing, repeat the washings until the water remains clear, or replace the cloth with another fabric. If fabrics are wrinkled after washing and drying, iron them before using them.

Fabrics suitable for quilting are generally lightweight, tightly woven cotton and cotton/polyester blends. They should not unravel easily and should not hold excessive wrinkles when squeezed and released. Because of the hours of time required to make a quilt, it is worth investing in high quality fabrics.

Fabric requirements given here are for standard 45″ wide fabric. If you use wider or more narrow fabrics, calculate the variations you will need.

All seams are sewn using ¼″ seam allowances. Measurements given include seam allowances, except for applique pieces (see "How to Applique" section).

Applique Quilts

Preparing Background Fabric

When you purchase fabric to be used for background and borders, it is best to buy the total amount you need from one bolt of fabric. This will assure that all the patches and borders will be the same shade. Dye lots can vary significantly from bolt to bolt of fabric, and those differences are emphasized when placed next to each other in a quilt top.

Cutting diagrams in the book are shown to make the most efficient use of fabric. Label each piece after it is cut. Mark right and wrong sides of fabric as well.

So that you know where to place the applique pieces on the background piece, trace the applique design lightly on the right side of the background fabric before beginning to stitch. Even though the applique will be laid over these markings and stitched in place, it is important to mark these lines as lightly as possible. Center the applique designs on the background sections. The placement of the applique on the pillow throw is an exception to that rule. Center that applique from side to side, but place it nearer the top of the quilt so that there is extra fullness for tucking the quilt under the pillows. The space from the top of the pillow throw section to the highest point of the applique design should measure about 10 inches.

Making Templates

Make templates from pattern pieces printed in this book, using material that will not wear along the edges from repeated tracing. Cardboard is suitable for pieces being traced only a few times. Plastic lids or the sides of plastic cartons work well for templates that will be used repeatedly. Quilt supply shops and art supply stores carry sheets of plastic that work well for template-making.

Quiltmaking demands precision. Remember that as you begin marking. First, test the template you have made against the original printed pattern for accuracy. The applique templates are given in their actual size, without seam allowances. Trace them that way. Then trace them on the right side of the fabric, but spaced far enough apart so that you can cut them approximately ¼" outside the marked line. The traced line is the fold line indicating the exact shape of the applique piece. Since these lines will be on the right side of the fabric and will be on the folded edge, markings should be as light as possible.

Each applique piece needs to be traced separately (rather than having the fabric doubled) so the fold line is marked on each one. However, since some of the pieces face in opposite directions, half should be traced one way and the other half should be traced the opposite way.

Appliqueing

Begin by appliqueing the cut-out fabric pieces, one at a time, over

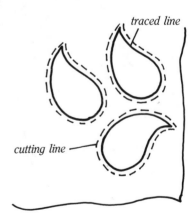

traced line

cutting line

Applique templates should be traced on the right side of the fabric but spaced far enough apart so they can be cut approximately ¼" outside the marked line.

The applique stitch is a tiny, tight stitch that goes through the background fabric and emerges to catch only a few threads of the appliqued piece along the fold line.

the placement lines drawn onto the background fabric pieces. Be alert to the sequence in which the pieces are appliqued, so that sections which overlay each other are done in proper order. In cases where a portion of an applique piece is covered by another, the section being covered does not need to be stitched, since it will be held in place by the stitches of the section that overlays it.

Appliqueing is not difficult, but it does require patience and precision. The best applique work has perfectly smooth curves and sharply defined points. To achieve this, stitches must be very small and tight. First, pin the piece being appliqued to the outline on the background piece. Using thread that matches the piece being applied, stitch the piece to the background section, folding the seam allowance under to the traced line on the applique piece. Fold under only a tiny section at a time.

The applique stitch is a running stitch going through the background fabric and emerging to catch only a few threads of the appliqued piece along the fold line. The needle should re-enter the background piece for the next stitch at almost the same place it emerged, creating a stitch so small that it is almost invisible along the edge of the appliqued piece. Stitches on the underside of the background fabric should be about $\frac{1}{8}''$ long.

To form sharp points, fold in one side and stitch almost to the end of the point. Fold in the opposite side to form the point and push the excess seam allowance under with the point of the needle. Excess seam allowance may be trimmed to eliminate bulk. Stitch tightly.

To form smooth curves, clip along the curves to the fold line. Fold under while stitching, using the needle to push under the seam allowances.

Assembling the Appliqued Quilt Top

When all applique work is completed, the patches are ready to be assembled. See the diagrams on pages 15 through 20.

Quilting on Applique and Pieced Quilts
Marking Quilting Designs

Quilting designs are marked on the surface of the quilt top. A lead pencil provides a thin line and, if used with very little pressure, creates markings that are easily seen for quilting, yet do not distract when the quilt is completed. There are numerous marking pencils on the market, as well as chalk markers. Test whatever you choose on a scrap piece of fabric to be sure it performs as promised. Remember, quilting stitches do not completely cover quilting lines, so the lines should be light or removable.

Patterns for quilting designs are included in this book. Since most spread over several pages, you will need to assemble them before using them.

Quilting lines are marked on the surface of the quilt top. Markings should be as light as possible so they are easily seen for quilting, yet do not distract when the quilting is completed.

Quilting

A quilt consists of three layers—the back or underside of the quilt, the batting and the top, which is the appliqued layer. Quilting stitches follow a decorative pattern, piercing through all three layers of the quilt "sandwich" and holding it together.

Many quilters prefer to stretch their quilts into large quilting frames. These are built so that the finished area of the quilt can be rolled up as work on it progresses. This type of frame allows space for several quilters to work on the same quilt and because of that is used at quilting bees. Smaller hoops can be used to quilt small sections at a time. If you use one of the smaller frames, it is important that you first spread the three layers smoothly and baste them securely to prevent puckering.

The quilting stitch is a simple running stitch. Quilting needles are called "betweens" and are shorter than "sharps," which are regular hand sewing needles. The higher the number, the smaller the needle. Many quilters prefer a size 8 or 9 needle.

Quilting is done with a single strand of quilting thread. Knot the thread and insert the needle through the top layer, about one inch away from the point where quilting should emerge on a marked quilting line. Gently tug the knot through the fabric so it is hidden between the layers. Bring the needle up through the quilt top, going through all layers of the quilt.

Keep one hand under the quilt to feel when the needle has successfully penetrated all layers and to help guide the needle back up to the surface. Your upper hand receives the needle and repeats the process. It is possible to stack as many as five stitches on the needle before pulling the thread through. However, when you work curves, you have smoother results if you stack fewer stitches. Pull the quilting stitches taut but not so tight as to pucker the fabric. When you have used the entire length of thread, reinforce the stitching with a tiny backstitch. Reinsert the needle in the top layer, push it through for a long stitch, pull it out and clip it.

The goal in quilting is to have straight, even stitches that are of equal length on both the top and bottom of the quilt. Achieving that comes with hours of practice.

When you quilt on the applique patches, simply outline the applique designs. This outline quilting will accent the applique section and cause it to appear slightly puffed.

Binding

The final stage in completing a quilt is the binding, which finishes the quilt's raw edge. When binding a non-straightedged quilt, cut the binding strips on the bias. This allows more flex and stretch around curves. To cut on the bias, cut the fabric at a 45 degree angle to the straight of grain.

A double thickness of binding on the edge of the quilt gives it additional strength and durability. To create a double binding, cut the

A quilt is a sandwich of three layers—the quilt back, batting and the quilt top—all held together by the quilting stitches.

Mitering Corners

Step 1

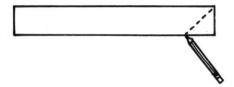

Measure in from each end the exact number of inches as the border width. Draw a diagonal line from that point to the outer corner. Cut along angled line.

Step 2

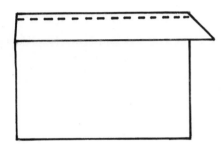

Stitch borders to quilt, leaving a ¼″ seam allowance open at each mitered end.

Step 3

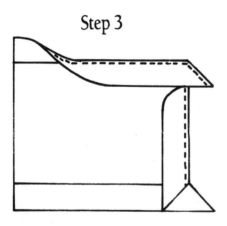

Stitch across the open ends of the corners from the inside corner to the outer edge.

binding strips 2-2½″ wide. Sew strips together to form a continuous length of binding.

When binding a quilt with scalloped edges, attach the binding before cutting the scalloped edge. To do so, baste the raw edges of the quilt together. Mark, but do not cut, the scalloped border. Fold binding strips in half length-wise with wrong sides together. Pin binding to quilt, having raw edges of binding and scalloped edge of quilt even. Using a ¼″ seam allowance, sew the binding along the marked edge, stitching through all the thicknesses. Trim the scallops even with the edge of the binding. Wrap the binding around to the back, enclosing the raw edges and covering the stitch line. Slipstitch in place with thread that matches the color of the binding fabric.

To Display Quilts

Wall quilts can be hung in various ways. You can simply tack the quilt directly to the wall. However, this is potentially damaging to both quilt and wall. Except for a permanent hanging, this is probably not the best way.

Another option is to hang the quilt like a painting. To do this, make a narrow sleeve from matching fabric and handsew it to the upper edge of the quilt along the back. Insert a dowel rod through the sleeve and hang the rod by wire or nylon string.

The quilt can also be hung on a frame. This method requires velcro or fabric to be attached to the frame itself. If you choose velcro, staple one side to the frame. Handsew the opposite velcro on the edge of the quilt, then attach the quilt carefully to the velcro on the frame. If you attach fabric to the frame, handstitch the quilt to the frame itself.

Quilts can also be mounted inside plexiglas by a professional framery. This method, often reserved for antique quilts, can provide an acid-free, dirt-free and, with special plexiglas, a sun-proof environment for your quilt.

Other Projects

The Country Bride *Collection* patterns are adaptable to other projects as well. To make a wall hanging, follow the instructions for appliqueing, but use only one square patch, and then add a border with decorative quilting. Borders on wall hangings may be mitered for a more tailored look. See illustration for instructions on mitered corners.

Pillows can also be made using a single patch. Applique the pillow top and quilt the patch. To make the back of the pillow, cut a square equal in size to the front in either matching or contrasting fabric.

Make a ruffle using one of the fabrics used in the applique design. To make the ruffle, cut three strips of fabric measuring 4½″ x 45″ each. Sew these strips together to form a continuous length. Bring the two ends together, with right sides together, and stitch to create a fabric circle. Fold the fabric circle in half lengthwise with wrong sides together. Stitch along the raw edge with a long running stitch the entire circumference of the circle. Gather the circle to fit around the edges of the quilted top. Pin the ruffle to the pillow top with raw edges even and spreading gathers evenly throughout. Baste ruffle to pillow top.

With right sides together and a ruffle sandwiched between the layers, pin back to pillow top. Stitch back to top through all layers, leaving a five-inch opening along one side. Trim seams. Turn pillow right side out. Stuff pillow with polyester fiberfil. Slipstitch opening.

Signing and Dating Quilts

To preserve history for future generations, sign and date the quilts you make. Include your initials and the year the quilt was made. Traditionally this data is added discreetly in a corner of the quilt. It can be embroidered or quilted among the quilting designs. Another alternative is to stitch or write the information on a separate piece of fabric and handstitch it to the back of the quilt. Whatever method you choose, this is an important part of finishing a quilt.

Applique Templates Needed to Complete Each Quilt in the Country Bride Collection:

The Country Bridesmaid	The Country Courtship	The Country Romance	The Country Wedding Wreath	The Country Trousseau
• Large Bird • Medium Leaf • Medium Tulip • Large Tulip • Alternate Heart Patch *Embroidered berries*	• Large Bird • Medium Leaf • Medium Heart Fan • Medium Tulip • Trip-Around-The-World Alternate Patches	• Small Bird • Small Tulip • Small Leaf • Tiny Heart Fan • Sashing *Embroidered berries*	• Large Bird • Medium Leaf • Large Tulip • Medium Tulip • Daisy • Berries • Bow	• Medium Bird • Medium Leaf • Medium Tulip • Large Heart Fan • Alternate Heart Patch • Corner Triangles

Pillow Throw Applique Templates
(Needed for all Quilts)

• Pillow Throw Bird	• Small Tulip
• Small Leaf	• Small Heart Fan

Fabric Requirements for Applique Pieces for Each Quilt in the Country Bride Collection:

The Country Bridesmaid	The Country Romance	The Country Wedding Wreath	The Country Courtship	The Country Trousseau
10 Large Birds/2 Pillow Throw Birds—⅝ yard	18 Small Birds/ 2 Pillow Throw Birds—½ yard	2 Large Birds/2 Pillow Throw Birds—¼ yard	10 Large Birds/2 Pillow Throw Birds—⅝ yard	10 Medium Birds/2 Pillow Throw Birds—½ yard
10 Large Bird Wings/2 Pillow Throw Wings—⅜ yard	18 Small Bird Wings/2 Pillow Throw Bird Wings—¼ yard	2 Large Bird Wings/2 Pillow Throw Bird Wings—⅛ yard	10 Large Bird Wings/ 2 Pillow Throw Wings—⅜ yard	10 Medium Bird Wings/2 Pillow Throw Bird Wings—¼ yard
5 Large, 26 Medium, 3 Small Tulips—¾ yard	57 Small Tulips—⅝ yard	63 Medium, 16 Small Leaves—¾ yard	75 Medium, 16 Small Leaves—⅞ yard	102 Medium, 16 Small Leaves—1¼ yards
5 Large, 26 Medium and 3 Small Tulip Centers—⅜ yard	57 Small Tulip Centers—⅜ yard	4 Bows—⅜ yard	5 Medium, 3 Small Tulips—¼ yard	36 Medium, 3 Small Tulips—¾ yard
5 Large, 26 Medium and 3 Small Tulip Tips—⅛ yard	57 Small Tulip Tips—⅛ yard	1 Large, 60 Medium and 3 Small Tulips—1¼ yards	5 Medium, 3 Small Tulip Centers—⅛ yard	36 Medium, 3 Small Tulip Centers—⅜ yard
92 Medium and 16 Small Leaves—1⅛ yards	124 Small Leaves—⅞ yard	1 Large, 60 Medium and 3 Small Tulip Tips—¼ yard	5 Medium, 3 Small Tulip Tips—1/16 yard	36 Medium, 3 Small Tulip Tips—⅛ yard
16 Alternate Patch Hearts—⅝ yard	9 Tiny Heart Fans/1 Small Heart Fan—⅛ yard for hearts, ⅛ yard for each shade under heart	1 Large, 60 Medium and 3 Small Tulip Centers—½ yard	5 Medium, 1 Small Heart Fan—¼ yard for hearts, ⅛ yard for each shade under heart	5 Large, 1 Small Heart Fan—¼ yard for hearts, ⅛ yard for each shade under heart
16 Alternate Patch Inside Hearts—⅝ yard	Embroidery Floss or Bias Tape for Stems	48 Berries—⅛ yard	Embroidery Floss or Bias Tape for Stems	16 Alternate Patch Hearts—⅝ yard
1 Small Heart Fan—These small pieces can be cut using fabric left over from other templates.	Embroidery Floss for Berries	22 Daisies—½ yard	Embroidery Floss for Berries on Pillow Throw	16 Alternate Patch Inside Hearts—⅝ yard
Embroidery Floss or Bias tape for stems	Sashing (cut 2½″ strips)—3 yards	22 Daisy Centers—1/16 yard	Background Patches and Borders—8 yards	Embroidery Floss or Bias Tape for Stems
Embroidery Floss for Berries	Background Patches and Borders—9¼ yards	1 Small Heart Fan—These small pieces can be cut using fabric left over from other templates.	Quilt Back—6½ yards, plus section remaining from Side Borders	Embroidery Floss for Berries on Pillow Throw
Binding—1¼ yards	Binding—1¼ yards	Embroidery Floss or Bias Tape for Stems	Binding—1¼ yards	20 Contrasting Triangles on Applique Patches (Triangles measure 10¾″ x 10¾″ x 15¼″)—1 yard
Background Patches and Borders—9¼ yards	Quilt Back—6½ yards, plus section left over from Side Borders	Embroidery Floss for Berries	Fabric for Alternate Patches—1¾ yards divided among the number of fabrics used	Background Patches and Borders— 9 yards
Quilt Back—6¼ yards, plus 11″ remaining from Side Borders		Binding—1¼ yards		Binding—1¼ yards
		Background Patches and Borders—9 yards		Quilt Back—6½ yards, plus section left over from Side Borders
		Quilt Back—6½ yards, plus section remaining from Side Borders		(**NOTE:** Before beginning applique work, sew contrasting triangles to 15¼″ patch)

The Country Bride Collection Sampler Quilt may be done using any combination of designs and fabrics. Therefore, no specific fabric requirements are given.

The Country Bridesmaid Quilt
Cutting Lay-out for Queen-size or Double-Size Quilt

Final size—approximately 96" x 112"
Measurements include seam allowances

Total yardage for quilt top—9¼ yards
Total yardage for quilt back—6¼ yards
plus 11" remaining from cutting
borders of quilt top.

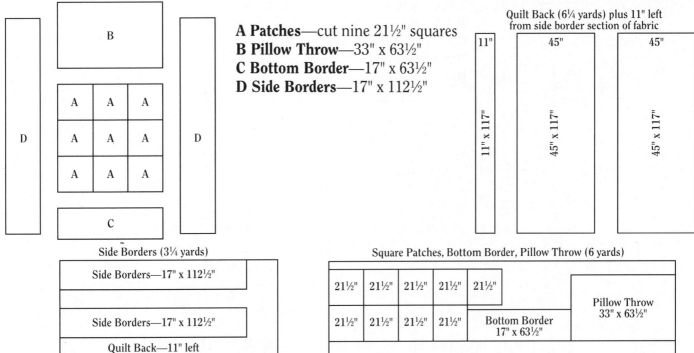

A Patches—cut nine 21½" squares
B Pillow Throw—33" x 63½"
C Bottom Border—17" x 63½"
D Side Borders—17" x 112½"

Quilt Back (6¼ yards) plus 11" left
from side border section of fabric

Side Borders (3¼ yards)

Side Borders—17" x 112½"

Side Borders—17" x 112½"

Quilt Back—11" left

Square Patches, Bottom Border, Pillow Throw (6 yards)

Assembly Instructions for the Country Bridesmaid Quilt
Queen-size/Double-size

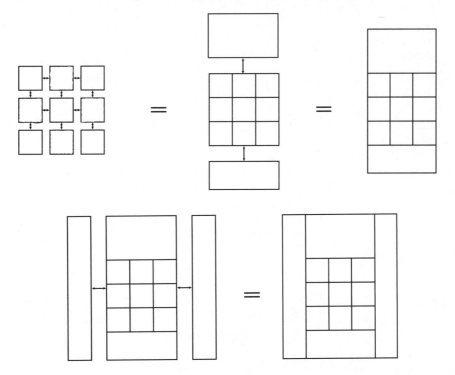

The Country Romance Quilt
Cutting Lay-out for Queen-size or Double-Size Quilt

Final size—approximately 96" x 112"
Measurements include seam allowances

Total yardage for quilt top—9¼ yards
Total yardage for quilt back—6¼ yards
plus 11" remaining from cutting
borders of quilt top.

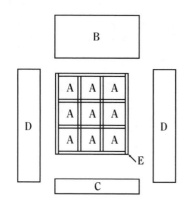

A Patches—cut nine 19½" squares
B Pillow Throw—33" x 63½"
C Bottom Border—17" x 63½"
D Side Borders—17" x 112½"
E Sashing—cut 2½" strips
(3 yards)

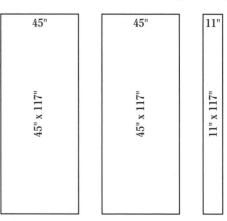

Square Patches, Bottom Border, Pillow Throw (5¾ yards)

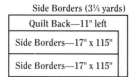

Side Borders (3¼ yards)

Quilt Back—11" left
Side Borders—17" x 115"
Side Borders—17" x 115"

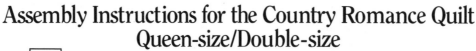

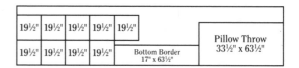

Assembly Instructions for the Country Romance Quilt
Queen-size/Double-size

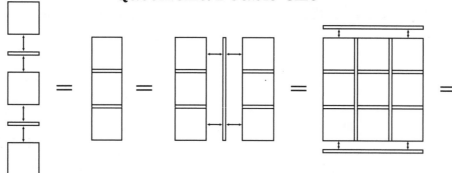

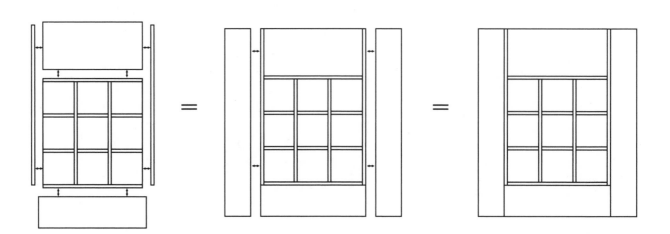

16

The Country Trousseau Quilt
Cutting Lay-out for Queen-size or Double-size Quilt

Final size—approximately 96" x 112"
Measurements include seam allowances

Total yardage for quilt top—9¼ yards
Total yardage for quilt back—6¼ yards
plus 11" remaining from cutting
borders of quilt top

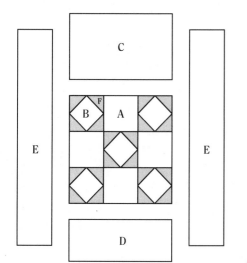

A Patches—cut four 21½" squares
B Patches—cut five 15¼" squares
C Pillow Throw—33" x 63½"
D Bottom Borders—17" x 63½"
E Side Borders—17" x 112½"
F Corner Triangles—
   10¾" x 10¾" x 15¼"
   (1 yard of contrasting fabric)

Quilt Back (6¼ yards) plus 11" left
from side border section of fabric

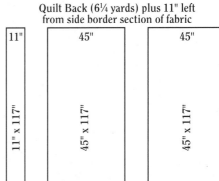

11"	45"	45"
11" x 117"	45" x 117"	45" x 117"

Side Borders (3¼ yards)

Side Borders—17" x 112½"
Side Borders—17" x 112½"
Quilt Back—11" left

Square Patches, Bottom Border, Pillow Throw (5¾ yards)

21½"	21½"	15¼" 15¼" 15¼"	Bottom Border 17" x 63½"	Pillow Throw 33" x 63½"
		15¼" 15¼"		
21½"	21½"			

Assembly Instructions for the Country Trousseau Quilt
Queen-size/Double-size

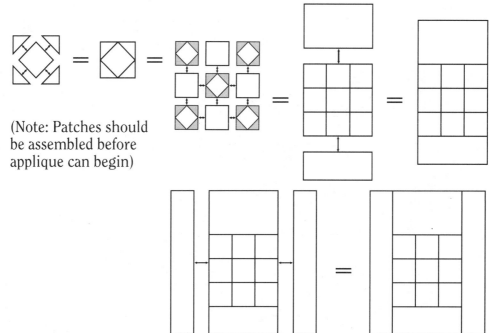

(Note: Patches should
be assembled before
applique can begin)

The Country Wedding Wreath Quilt
Cutting Lay-out for Queen-size or Double-Size Quilt

Final size—approximately 93" x 108"
Measurements include seam allowances

Total yardage for quilt top—9 yards
Total yardage for quilt back—6½ yards
plus 11" remaining from cutting
borders of quilt top.

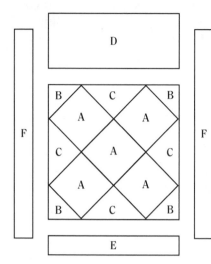

A Patches—cut five 21½" squares
B Corner Triangles—
—cut 4

C Corner Triangles—
—cut 4

D Pillow Throw—32½" x 60½"
E Bottom Border—17" x 60½"
F Side Borders—17" x 109"

Quilt Back (6¼ yards) plus 11" left from
side border section of fabric

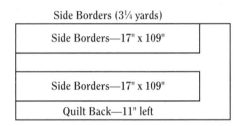

Square Patches, Bottom Border, Pillow Throw (5¾ yards)

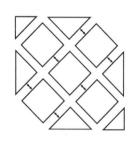
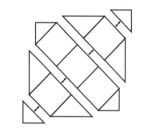

Side Borders (3¼ yards)

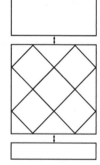

Assembly Instructions for the Country Wedding Wreath Quilt
Queen-size/Double-size

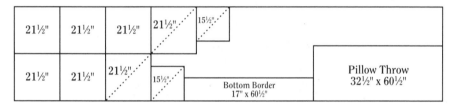

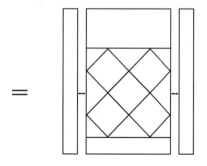
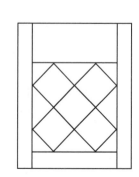

The Country Courtship Quilt
Cutting Lay-out for Queen-size or Double-Size Quilt

Final size—approximately 96" x 112"
Measurements include seam allowances

Total yardage for quilt top—8 yards
(Plus 1¾ yds. for alternate patches)
Total yardage for quilt back—6¼ yards
plus 11" remaining from cutting borders of quilt top.

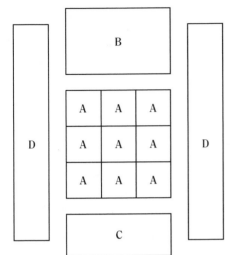

A Patches—cut five 21½" squares
B Pillow Throw—33" x 63½"
C Bottom Border—17" x 63½"
D Side Borders—17" x 112½"

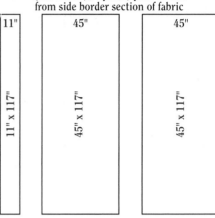

Quilt Back (6¼ yards) plus 11" left
from side border section of fabric

11" | 45" | 45"

11" x 117" | 45" x 117" | 45" x 117"

Square Patches, Bottom Border, Pillow Throw (4¾ yards)

21½" | 21½" | 21½" | 21½" | 21½"

Bottom Border
17" x 63½"

Pillow Throw
33" x 63½"

Side Borders (3¼ yards)

Side Borders—17" x 112½"

Side Borders—17" x 112½"

Quilt Back—11" left

Assembly Instructions for the
Around the World Alternate Patch

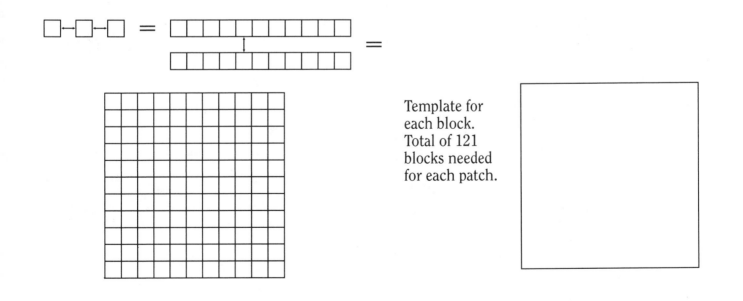

Template for
each block.
Total of 121
blocks needed
for each patch.

19

Assembly Instructions for the Country Courtship Quilt
Queen-size/Double-size

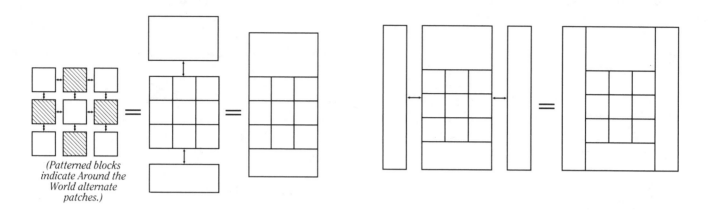

(Patterned blocks indicate Around the World alternate patches.)

Country Bride Collection Applique Templates

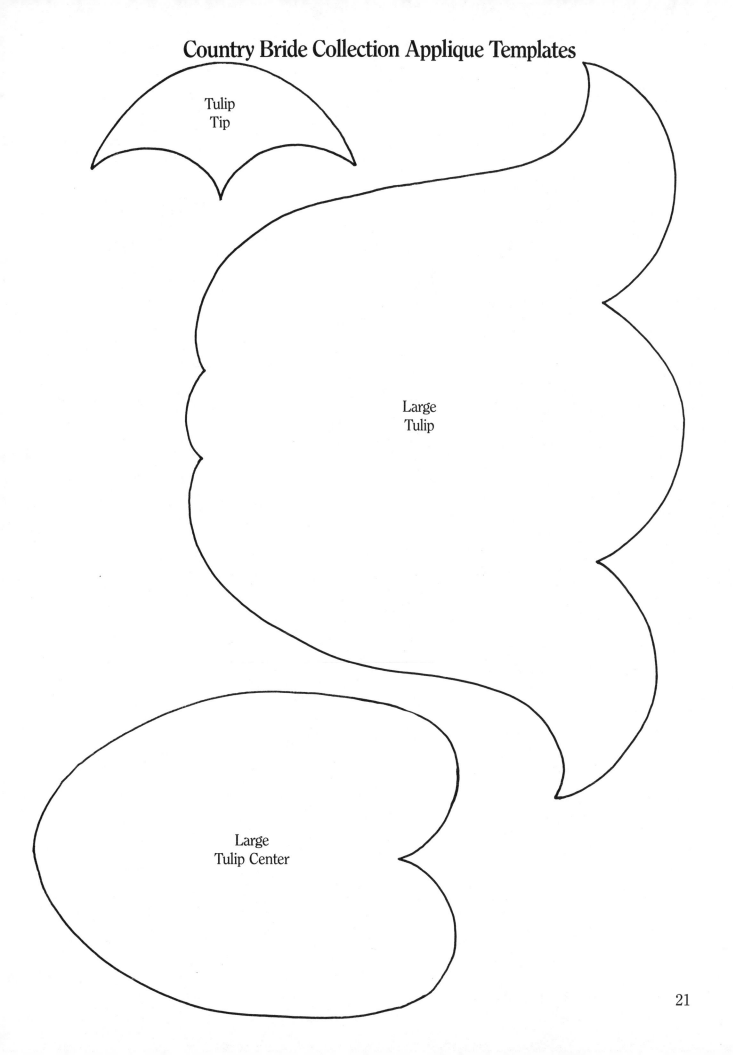

Tulip
Tip

Large
Tulip

Large
Tulip Center

Country Bride Collection Applique Templates

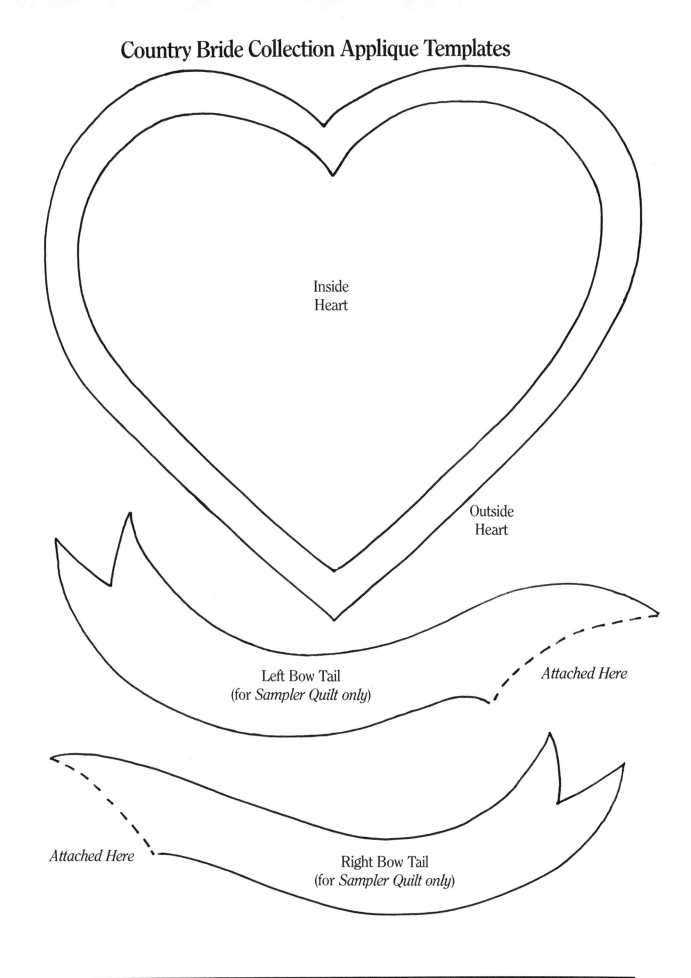

Inside
Heart

Outside
Heart

Left Bow Tail
(for *Sampler Quilt only*)

Attached Here

Attached Here

Right Bow Tail
(for *Sampler Quilt only*)

Country Bride Collection Applique Templates

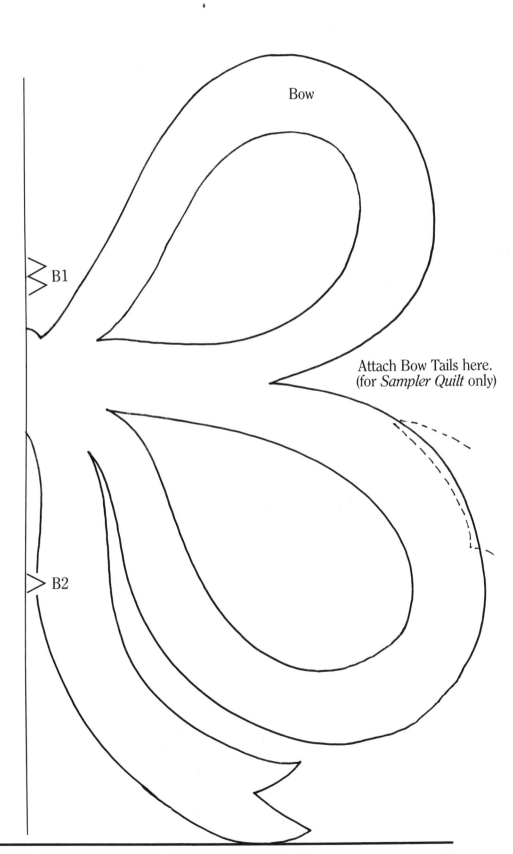

Bow

B1

Attach Bow Tails here.
(for *Sampler Quilt* only)

B2

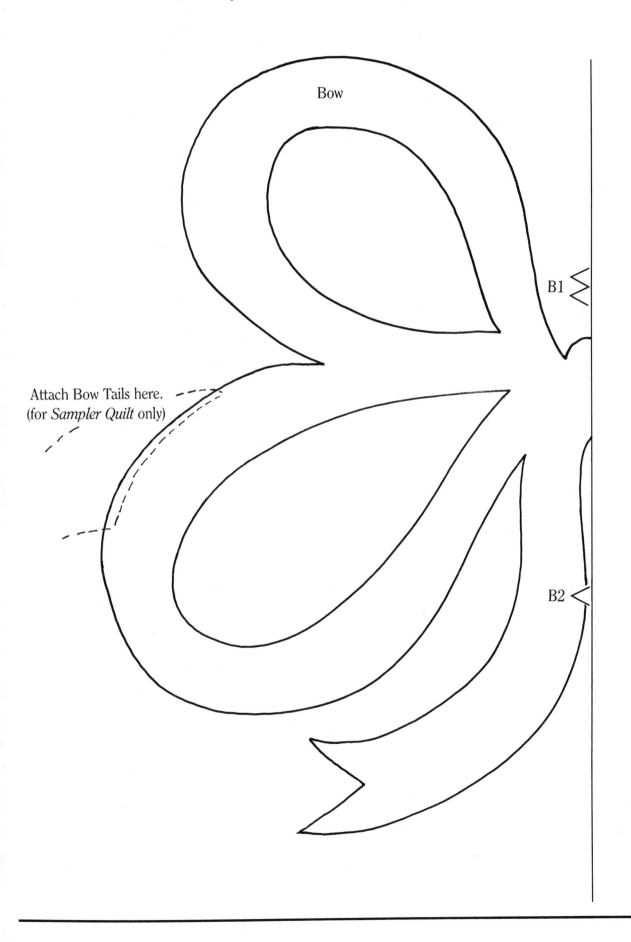

Bow

B1

Attach Bow Tails here.
(for *Sampler Quilt* only)

B2

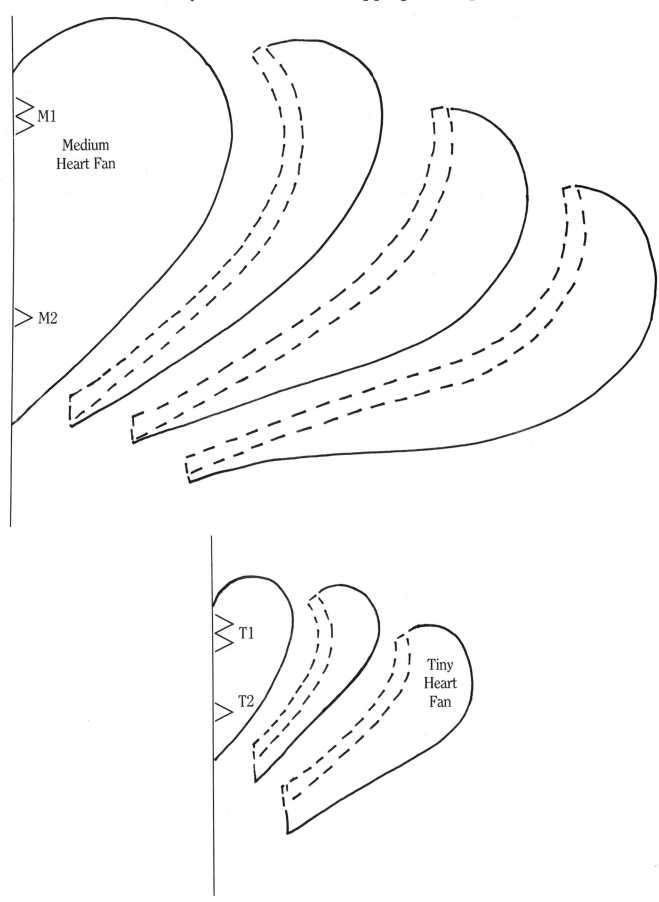

M1

Medium
Heart Fan

M2

T1

T2

Tiny
Heart
Fan

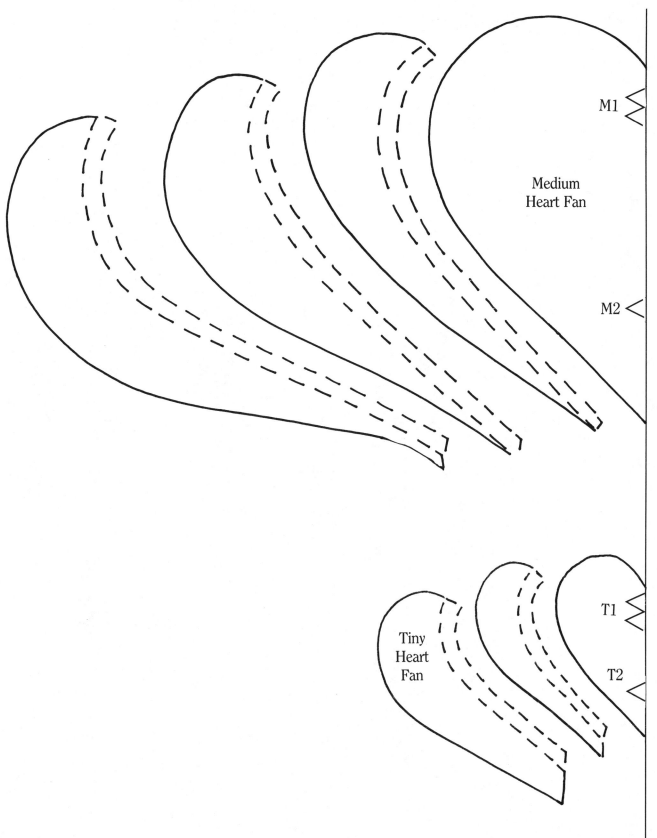

M1

Medium
Heart Fan

M2

Tiny
Heart
Fan

T1

T2

Country Bride Collection Applique Templates

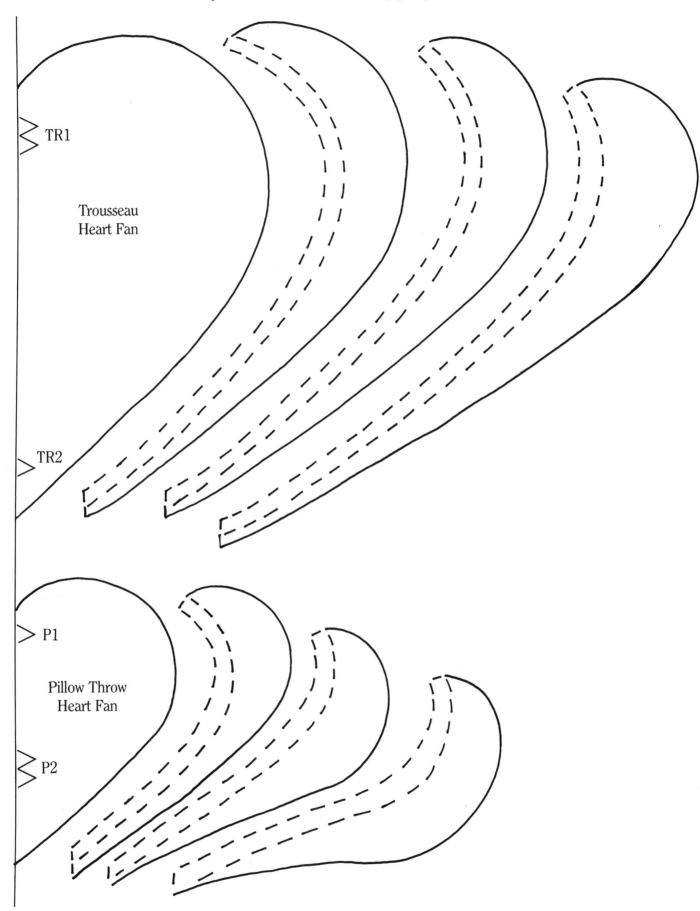

TR1

Trousseau
Heart Fan

TR2

P1

Pillow Throw
Heart Fan

P2

Country Bride Collection Applique Templates

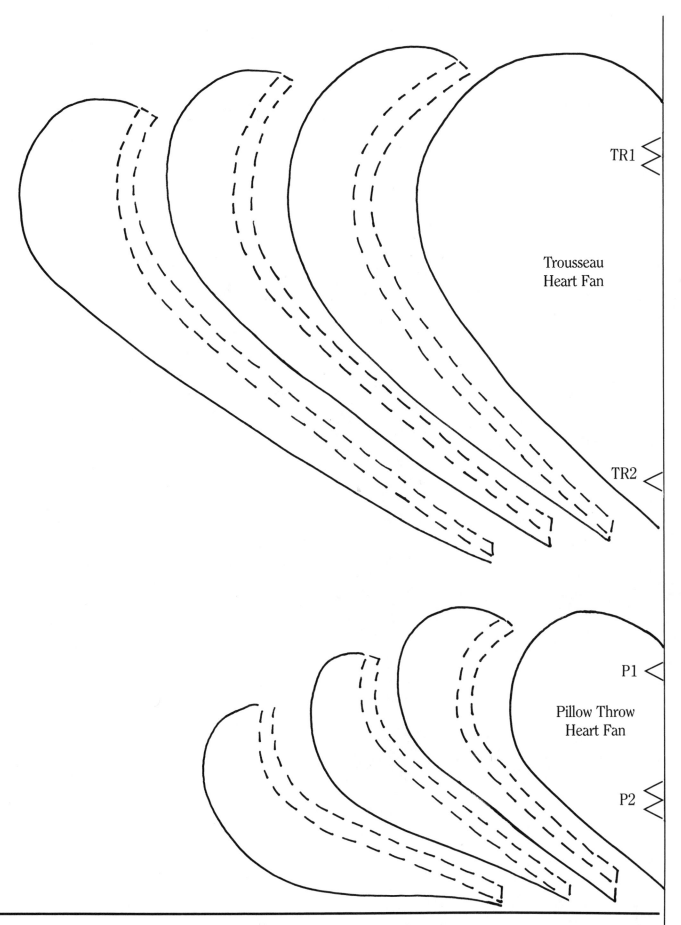

TR1

Trousseau
Heart Fan

TR2

P1

Pillow Throw
Heart Fan

P2

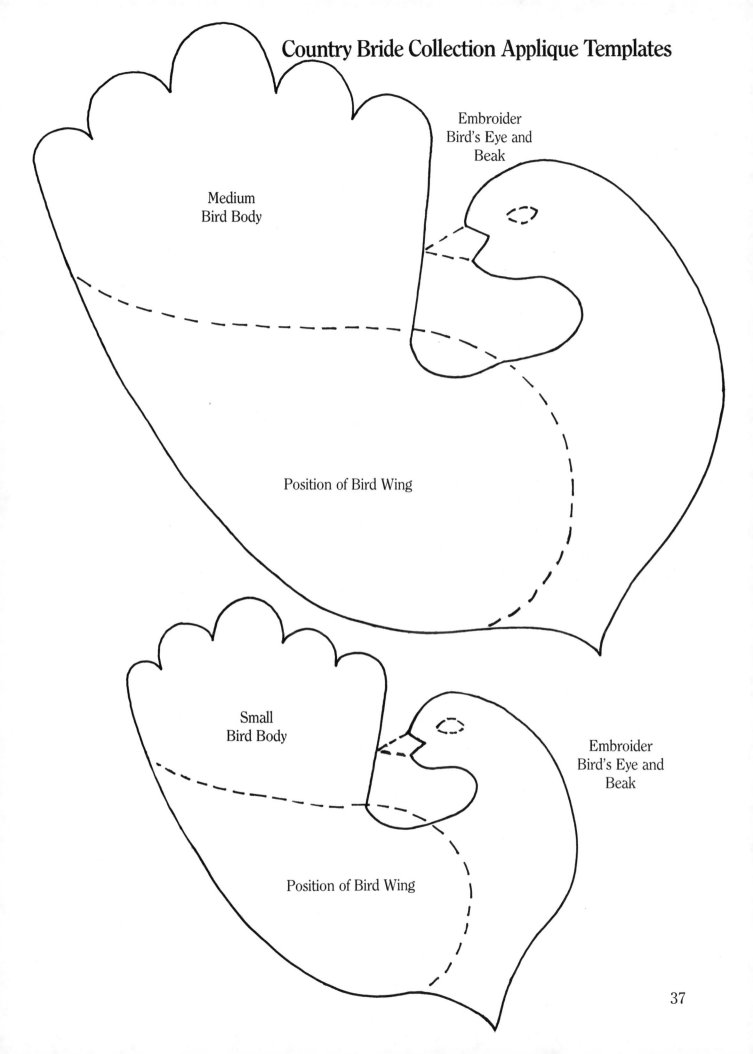

Country Bride Collection Applique Templates

Embroider
Bird's Eye and
Beak

Medium
Bird Body

Position of Bird Wing

Small
Bird Body

Embroider
Bird's Eye and
Beak

Position of Bird Wing

37

Country Bride Collection Applique Templates

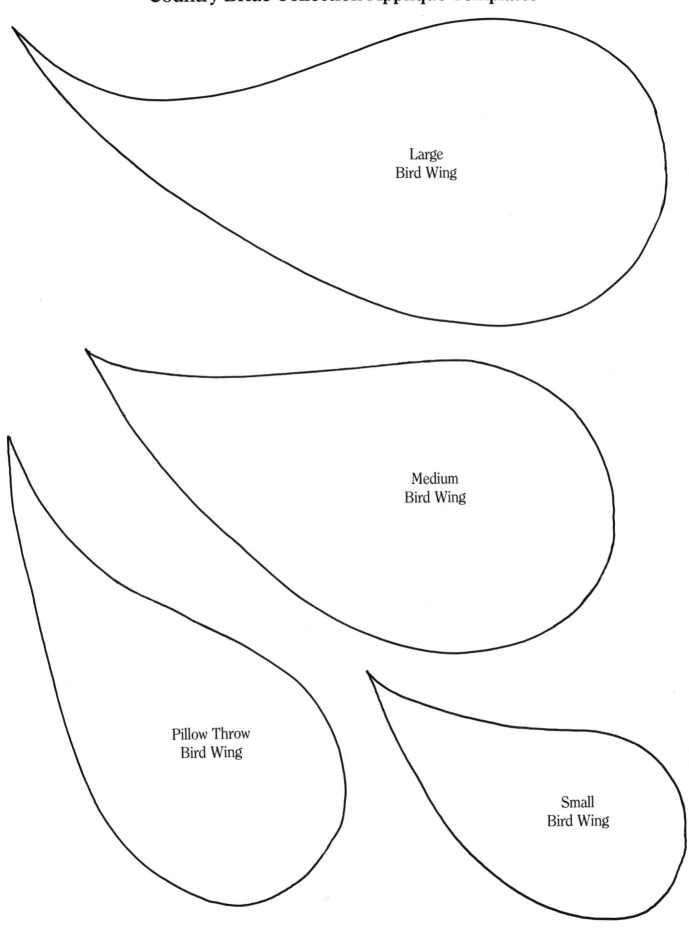

Large
Bird Wing

Medium
Bird Wing

Pillow Throw
Bird Wing

Small
Bird Wing

Country Bride Collection Applique Templates

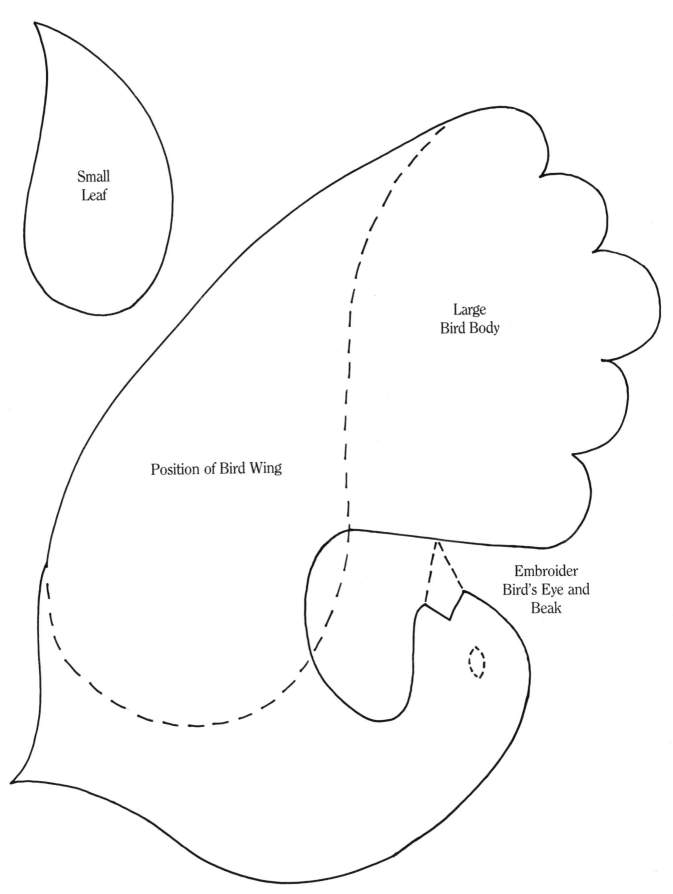

Small
Leaf

Large
Bird Body

Position of Bird Wing

Embroider
Bird's Eye and
Beak

Country Bride Collection Applique Templates

Tulip
Tip

Medium
Tulip Center

Medium
Tulip

Daisy Center
(also, Berry Template
for the *Wedding
Wreath* Patch)

Leaf

Daisy

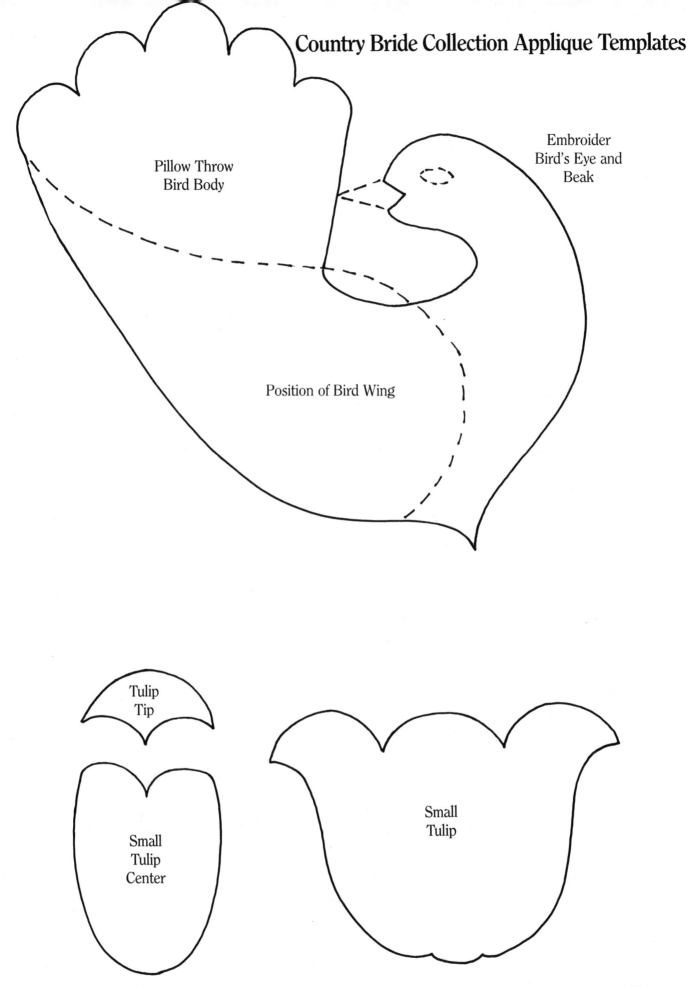

Pillow Throw
Bird Body

Embroider
Bird's Eye and
Beak

Position of Bird Wing

Tulip
Tip

Small
Tulip
Center

Small
Tulip

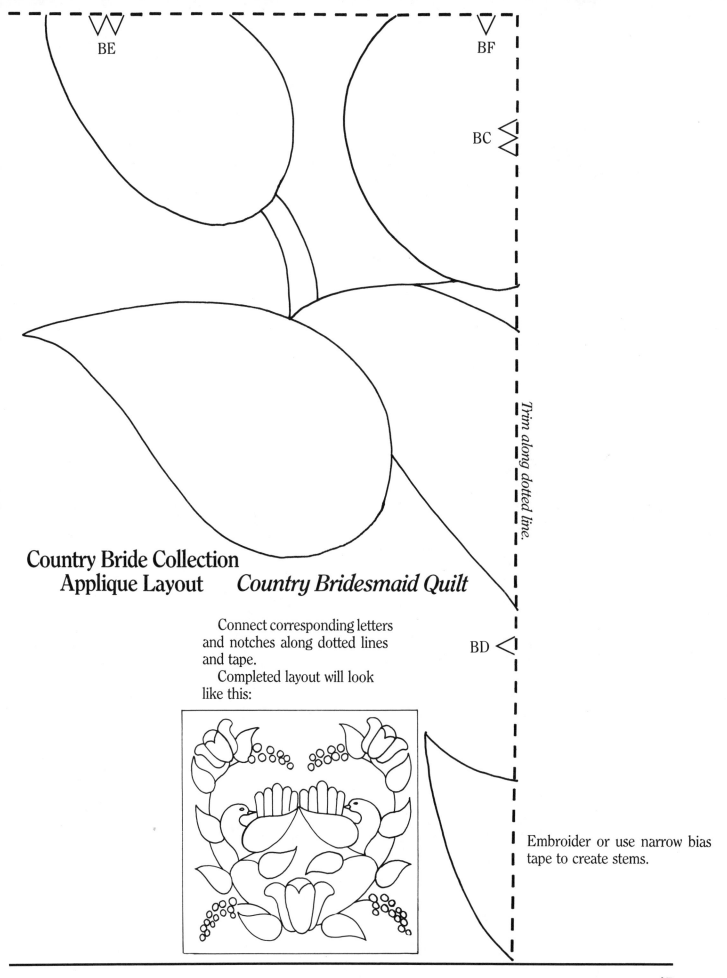

BE

BF

BC

BD

Country Bride Collection
Applique Layout   *Country Bridesmaid Quilt*

Connect corresponding letters
and notches along dotted lines
and tape.

Completed layout will look
like this:

Embroider or use narrow bias
tape to create stems.

Country Bride Collection Applique Layout
Country Bridesmaid Quilt

BO

BN

BL

BM

Trim along dotted line.

49

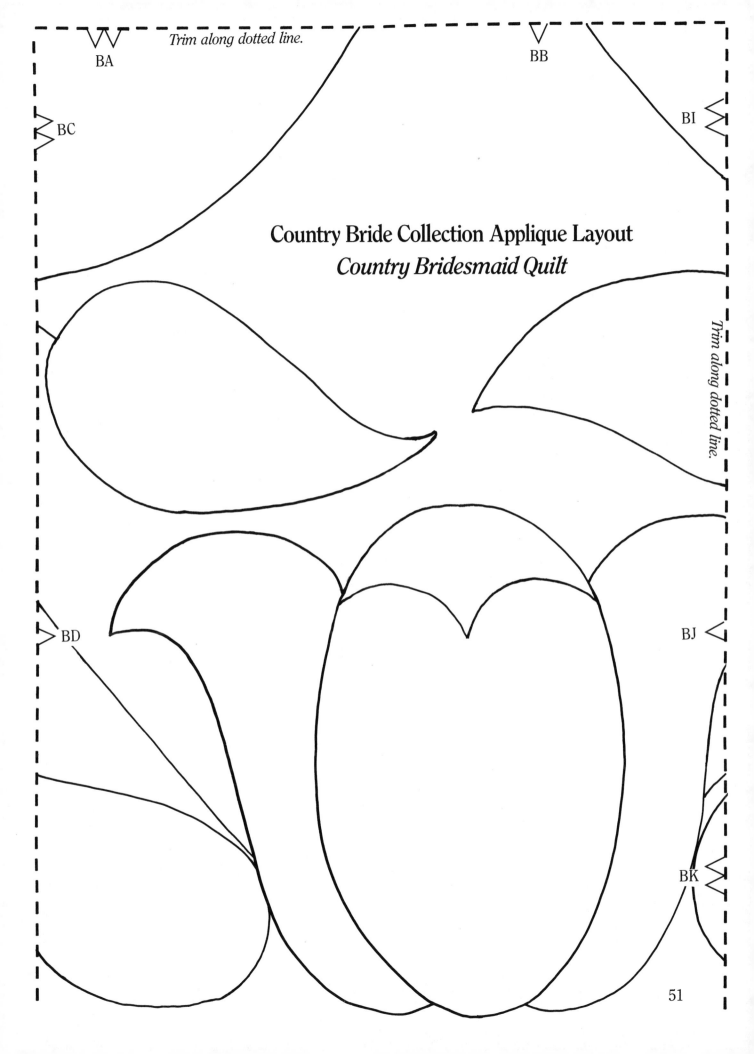

BA

BB

BI

BC

Country Bride Collection Applique Layout
Country Bridesmaid Quilt

BD

BJ

BK

51

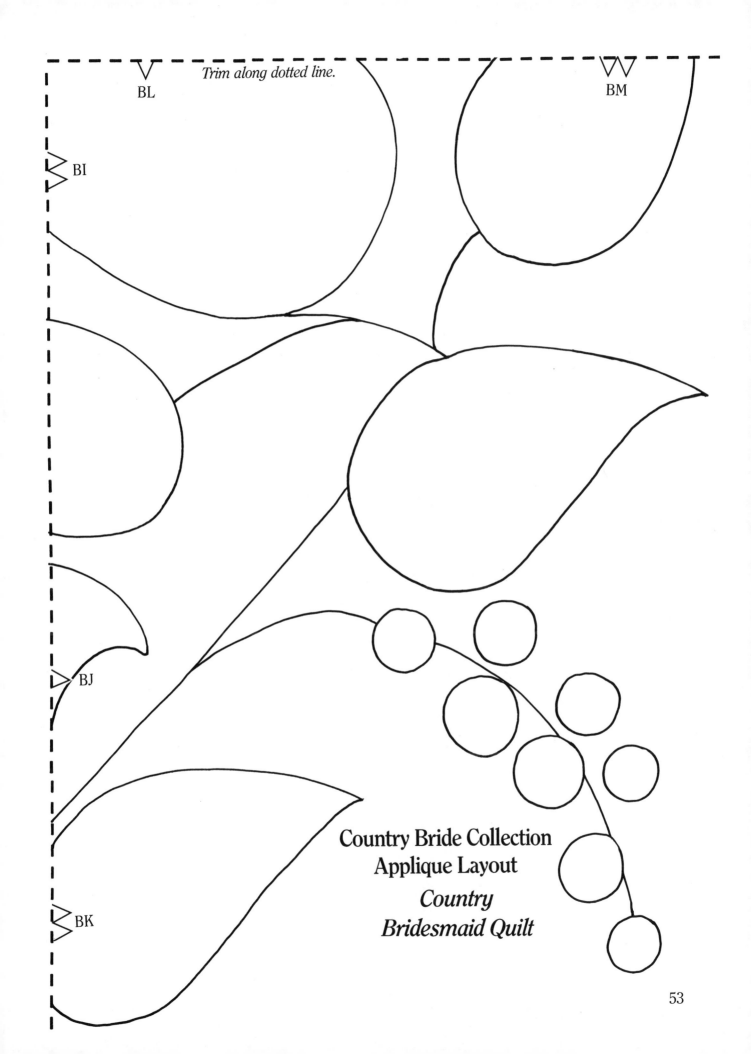

Trim along dotted line.

BL

BM

BI

BJ

BK

Country Bride Collection
Applique Layout
Country
Bridesmaid Quilt

53

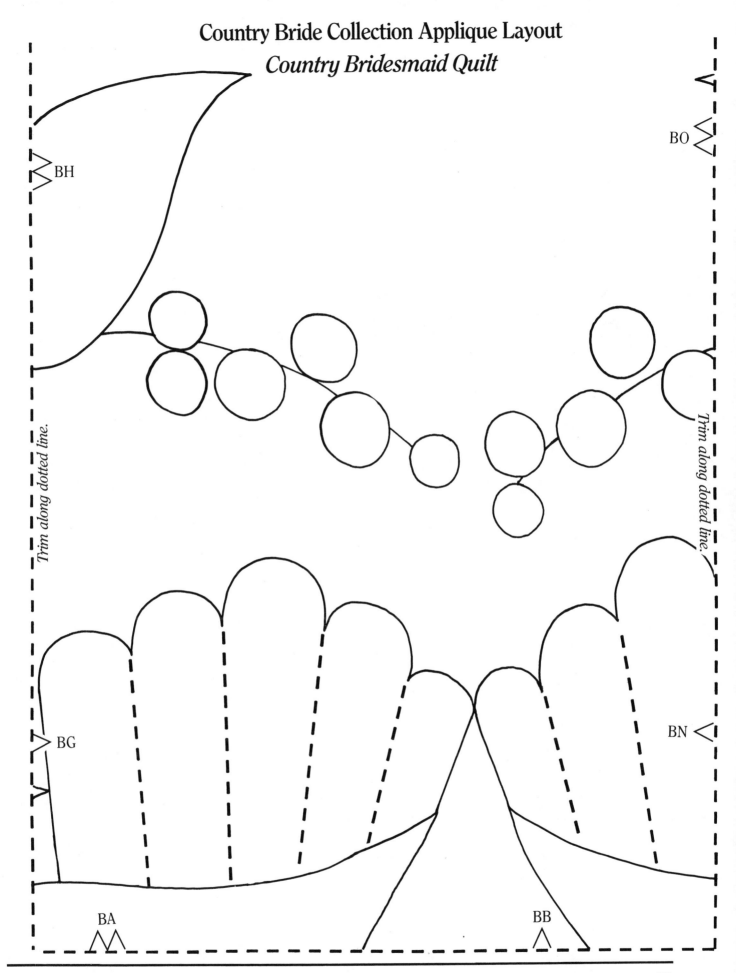

Trim along dotted line.

Trim along dotted line.

BH

BO

BG

BN

BA

BB

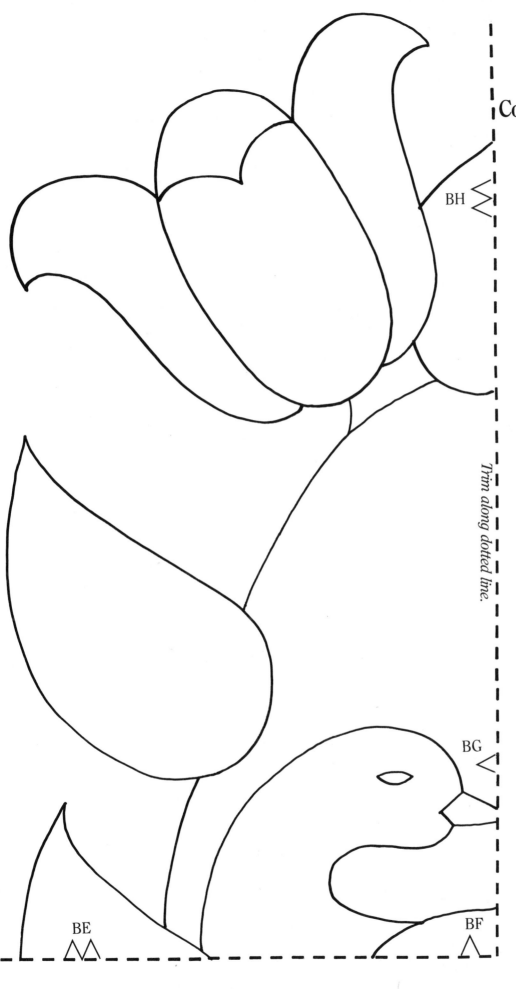

*Country
Bridesmaid Quilt*

BH

Trim along dotted line.

BG

BE

BF

Country Bride Collection Applique Layout
Country Trousseau Quilt

Connect corresponding letters
and notches along dotted lines
and tape.

Completed layout will look
like this:

Embroider or use narrow bias
tape to create stems.

Trim along dotted line.

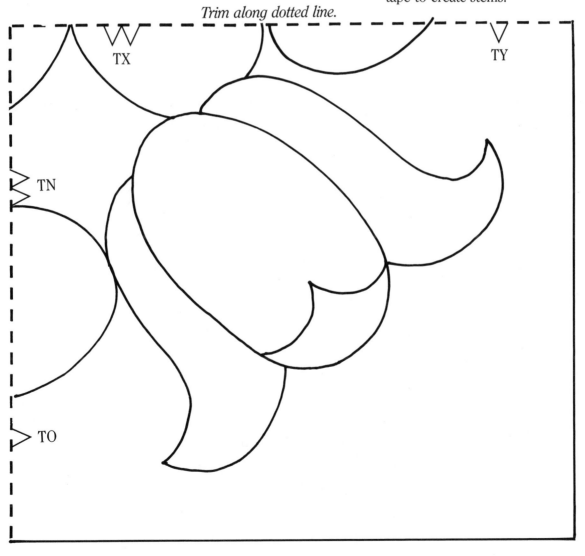

TX

TY

TN

TO

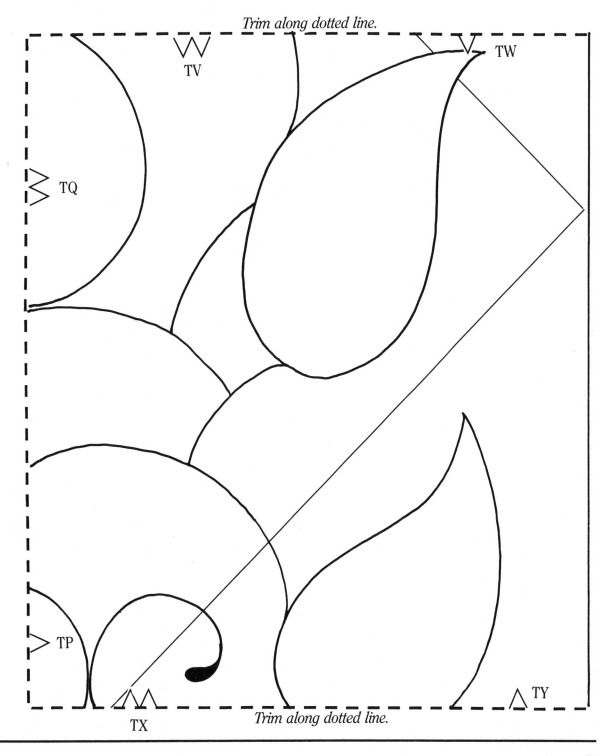

Trim along dotted line.

TV

TW

TQ

TP

TX

TY

Trim along dotted line.

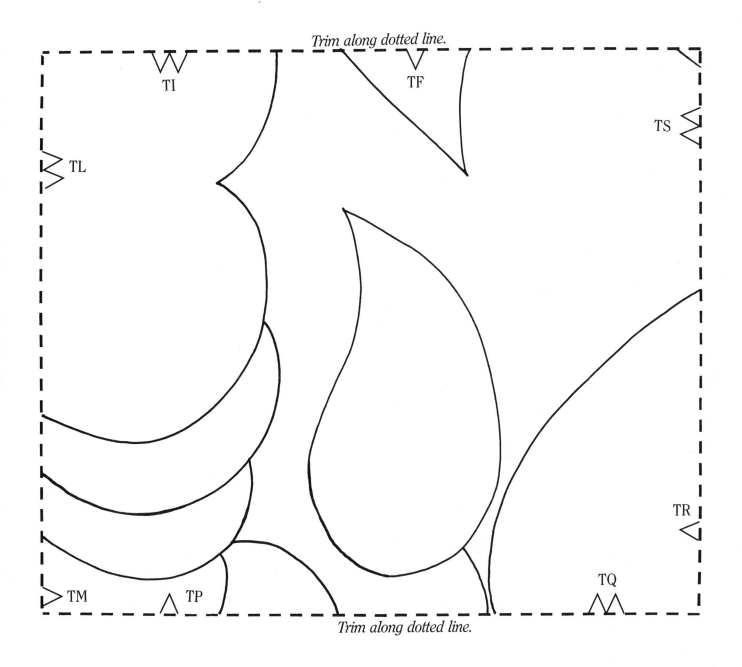

Trim along dotted line.

TI

TF

TS

TL

TR

TM

TP

TQ

Trim along dotted line.

Country Trousseau Quilt

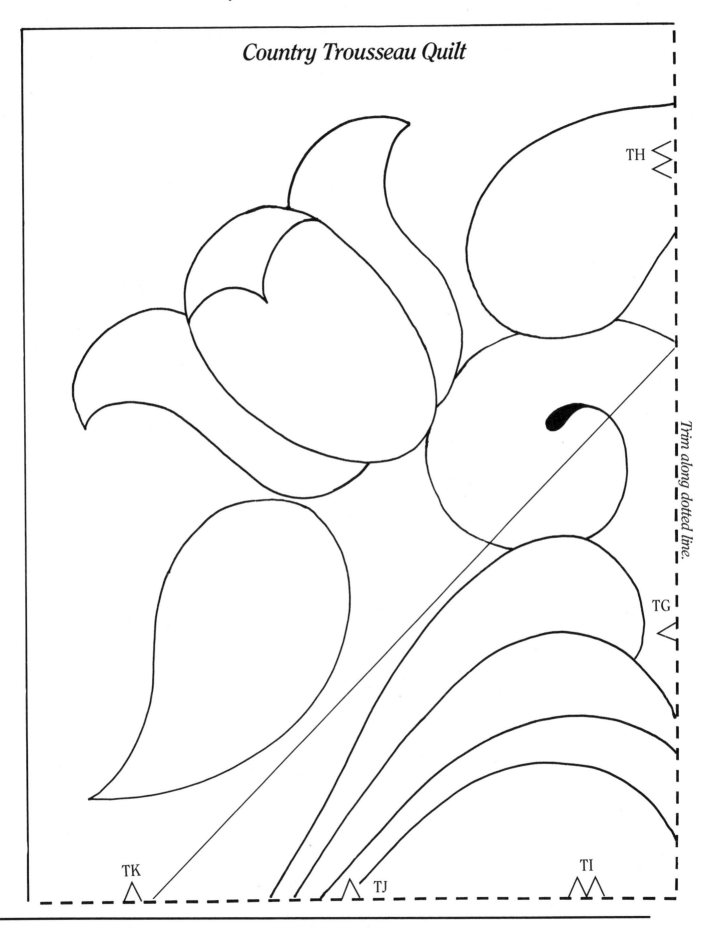

TH

TG

Trim along dotted line.

TK

TJ

TI

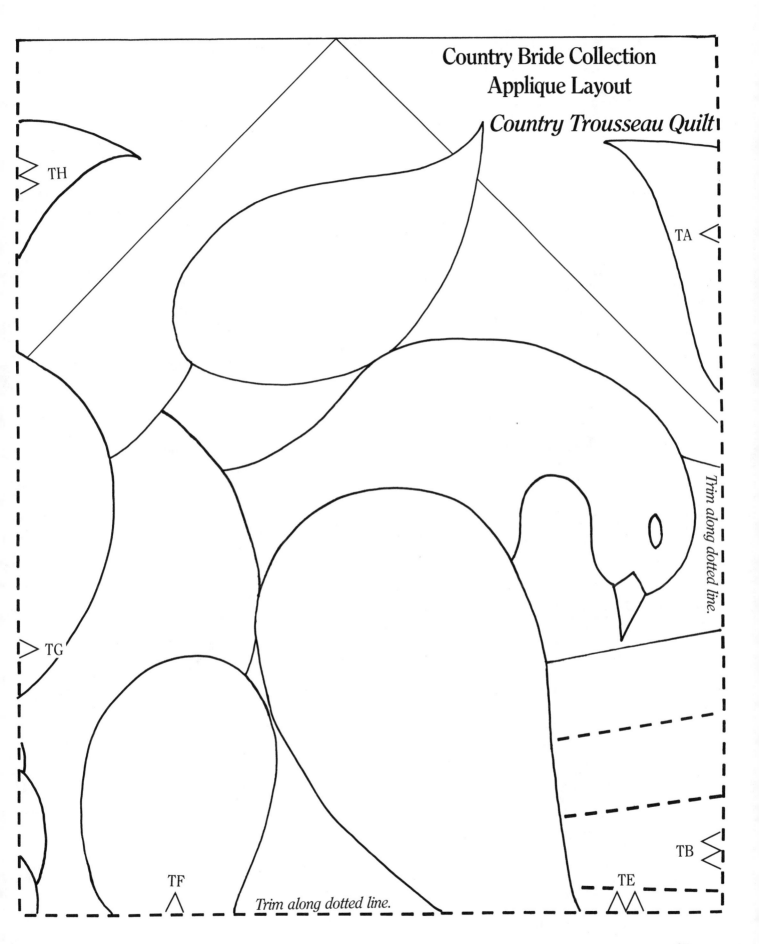

Country Bride Collection
Applique Layout

Country Trousseau Quilt

TH

TA

Trim along dotted line.

TG

TF

TB

TE

Trim along dotted line.

Country Trousseau Quilt

TA

TD

TB

Trim along dotted line.

TC

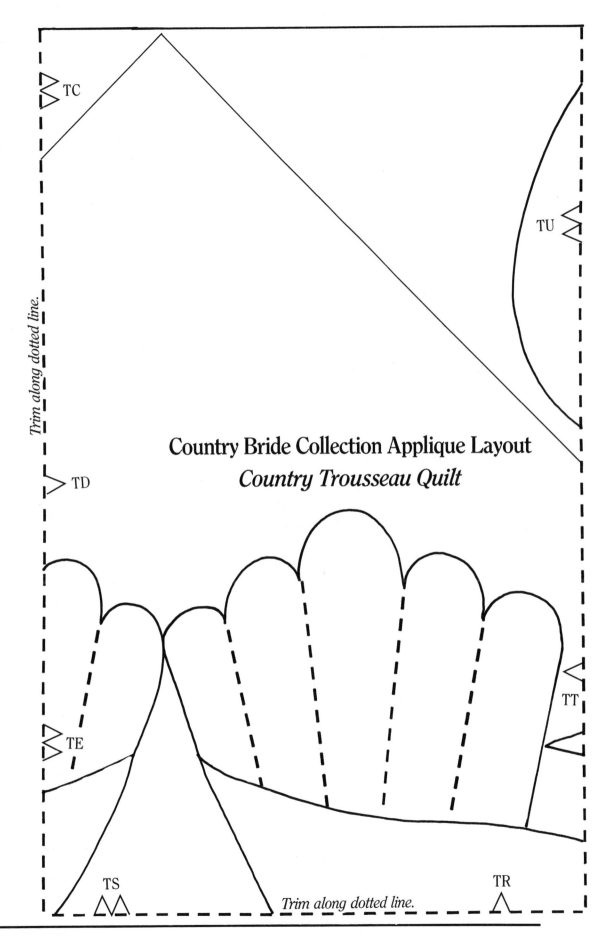

TC

TU

Trim along dotted line.

TD

Country Bride Collection Applique Layout
Country Trousseau Quilt

TT

TE

TS

TR

Trim along dotted line.

TU

TT

TV

TW

Trim along dotted line.

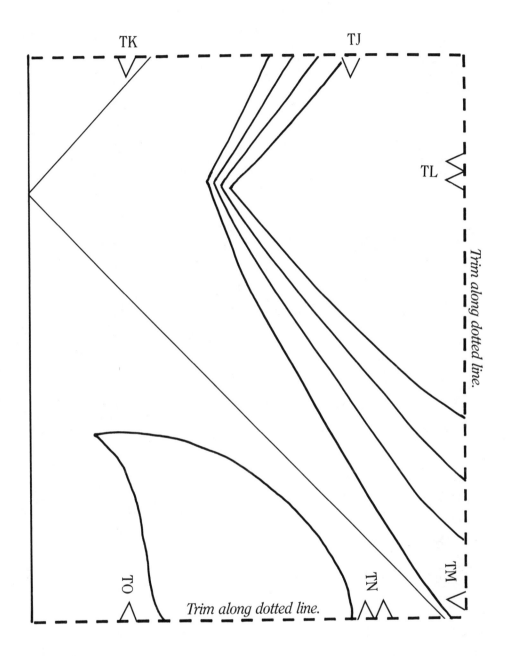

TK

TJ

TL

Trim along dotted line.

TO

Trim along dotted line.

TN

TM

Country Bride Collection Applique and Quilting Layout
Alternate Patch

Connect corresponding letters and notches along dotted lines and tape.

Completed layout will look like this:

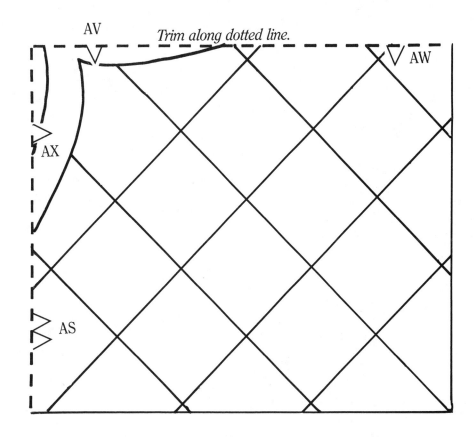

Country Bride Collection Applique and Quilting Layout
Alternate Patch

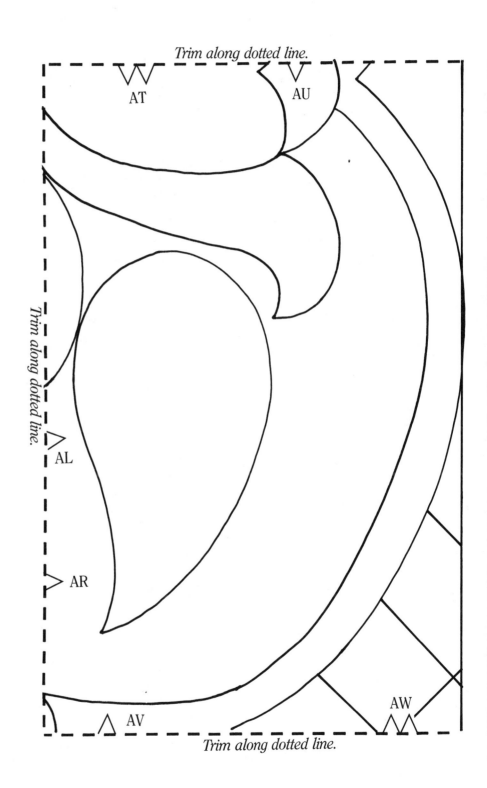

Trim along dotted line.

AT

AU

Trim along dotted line.

AL

AR

AV

AW

Trim along dotted line.

Country Bride Collection
Applique and Quilting Layout
Alternate Patch

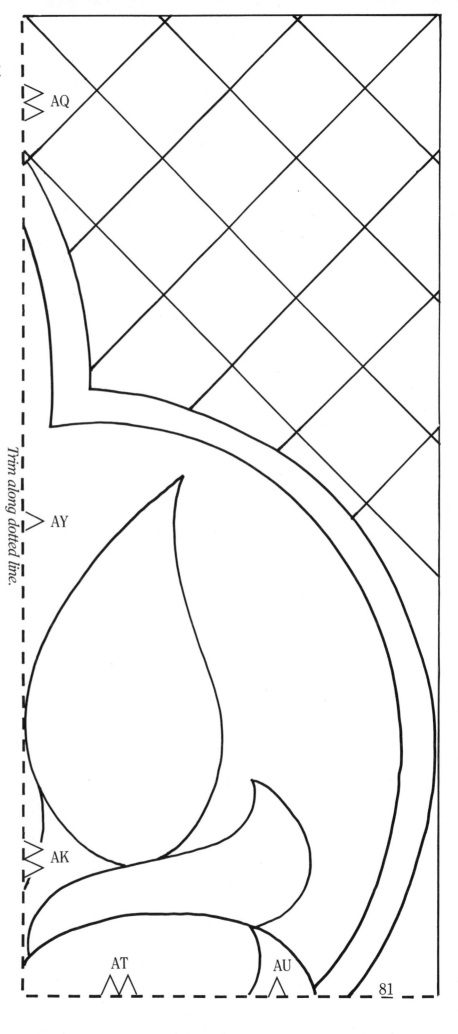

AQ

Trim along dotted line.

AY

AK

AT

AU

Country Bride Collection Applique and Quilting Layout

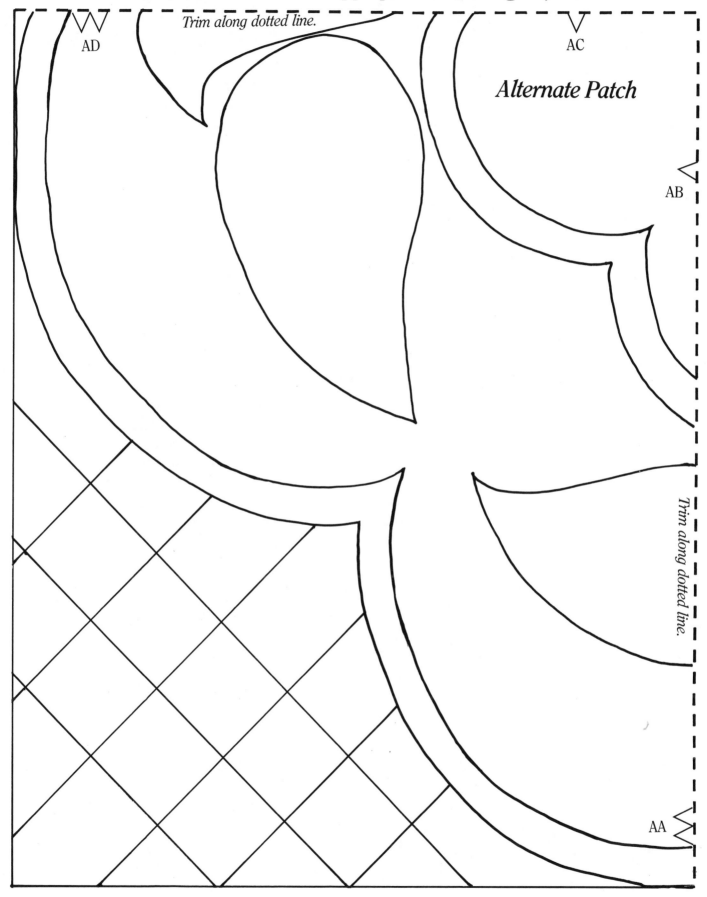

Trim along dotted line.

AD

AC

Alternate Patch

AB

Trim along dotted line.

AA

Country Bride Collection Applique and Quilting Layout
Alternate Patch

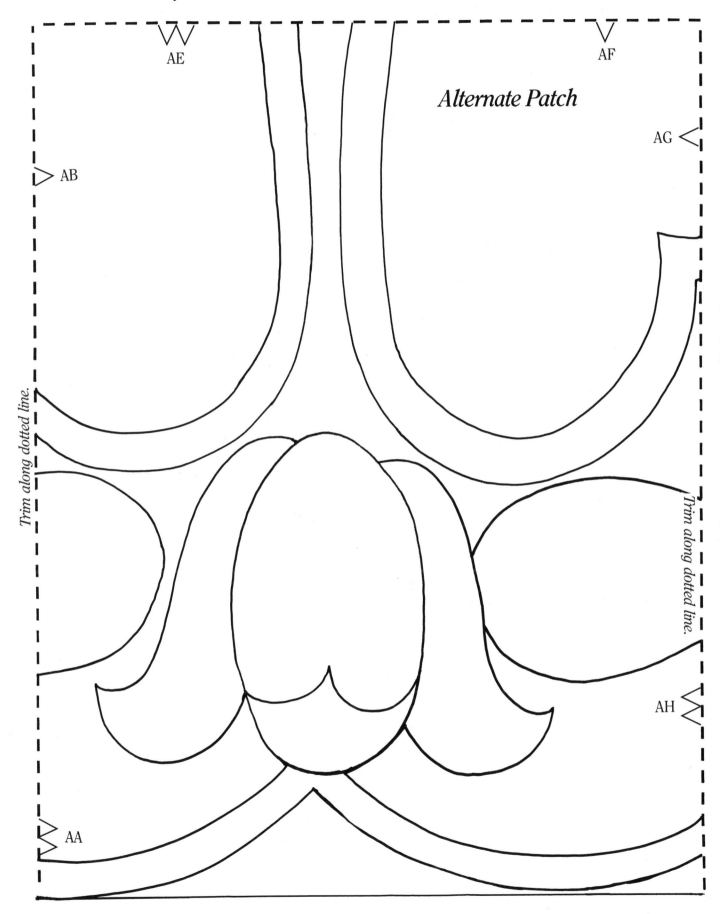

AE

AF

Alternate Patch

AG

AB

AH

Trim along dotted line.

Trim along dotted line.

AA

Trim along dotted line.

Trim along dotted line.

Country Bride Collection Applique and Quilting Layout
Alternate Patch

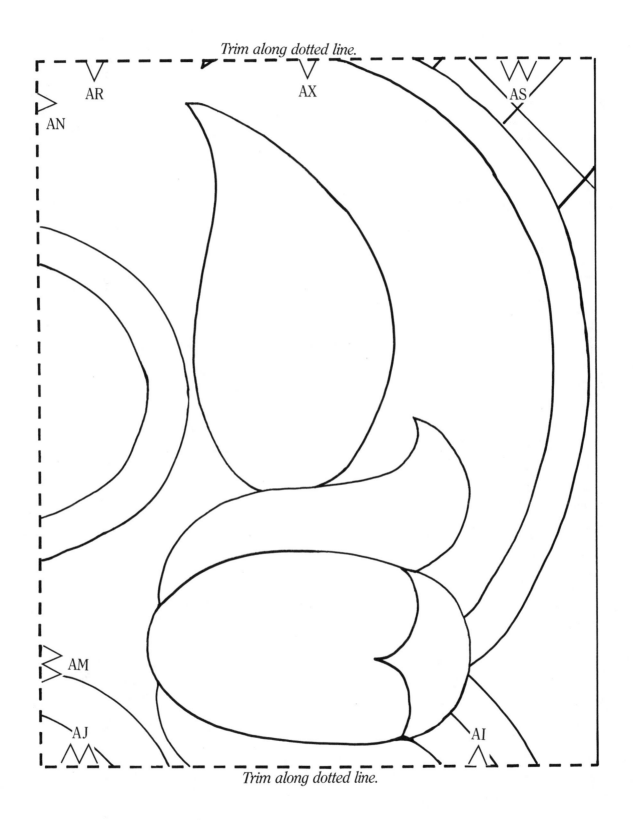

Trim along dotted line.

AR AX AS

AN

AM

AJ AI

Trim along dotted line.

Country Bride Collection Applique and Quilting Layout
Alternate Patch

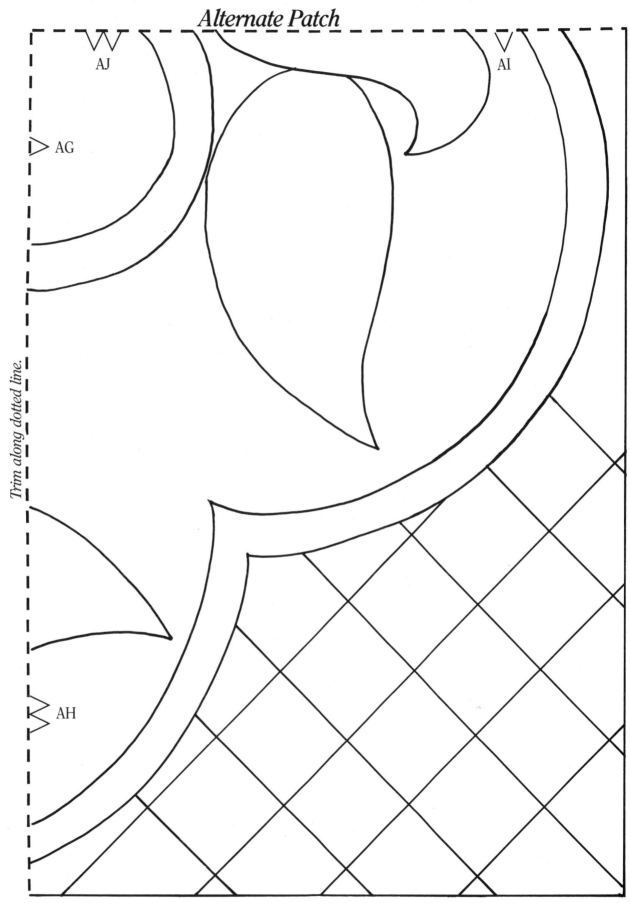

AJ

AG

AI

Trim along dotted line.

AH

Country Bride Collection Applique Layout
Country Romance Quilt

Connect corresponding letters and notches along dotted lines and tape.

Completed layout will look like this:

Trim along dotted line.

RH

RG

RF

RE

Trim along dotted line.

Country Bride Collection Applique Layout
Country Romance Quilt

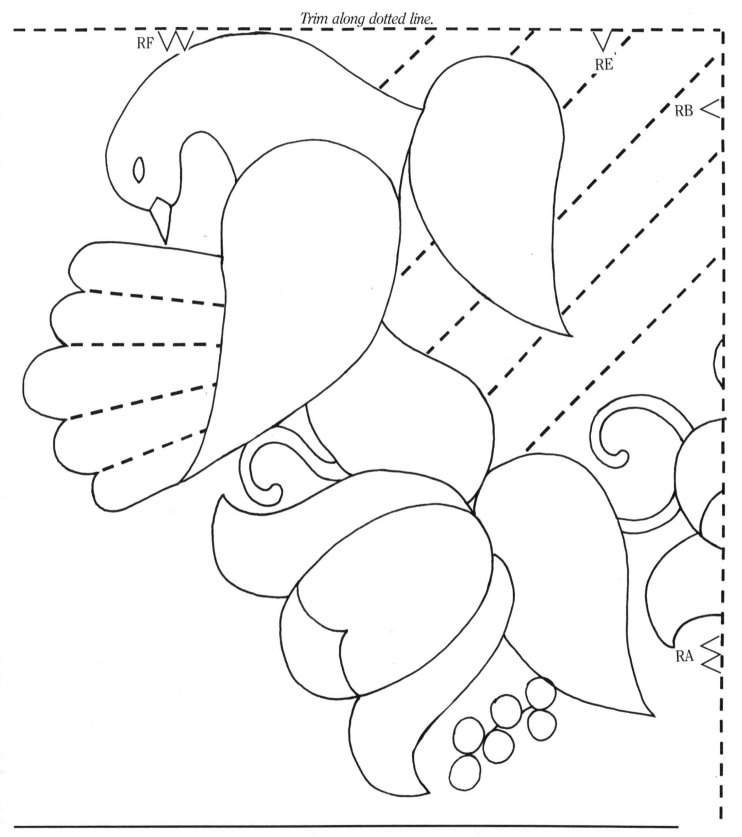

Trim along dotted line.

Country Bride Collection Applique Layout
Country Romance Quilt

Trim along dotted line.

RA

RB

RC

RD

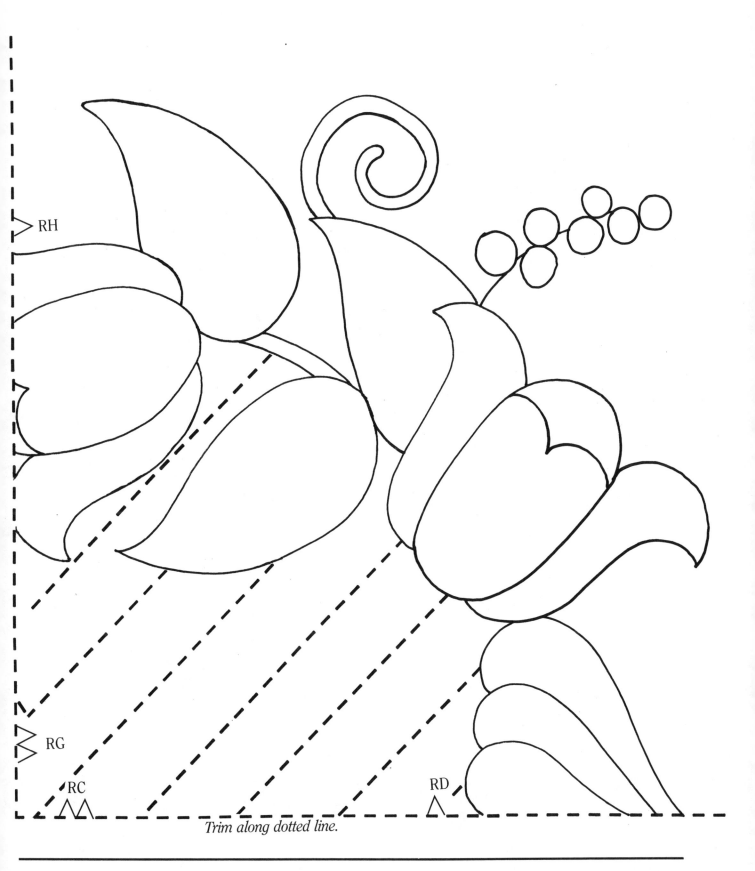

RH

RG

RC

RD

Trim along dotted line.

Country Romance Quilt
Sashing Template

Sashing appears
along the sides, top,
and between patches.
Quilt vine motif
within 2½" sashing.

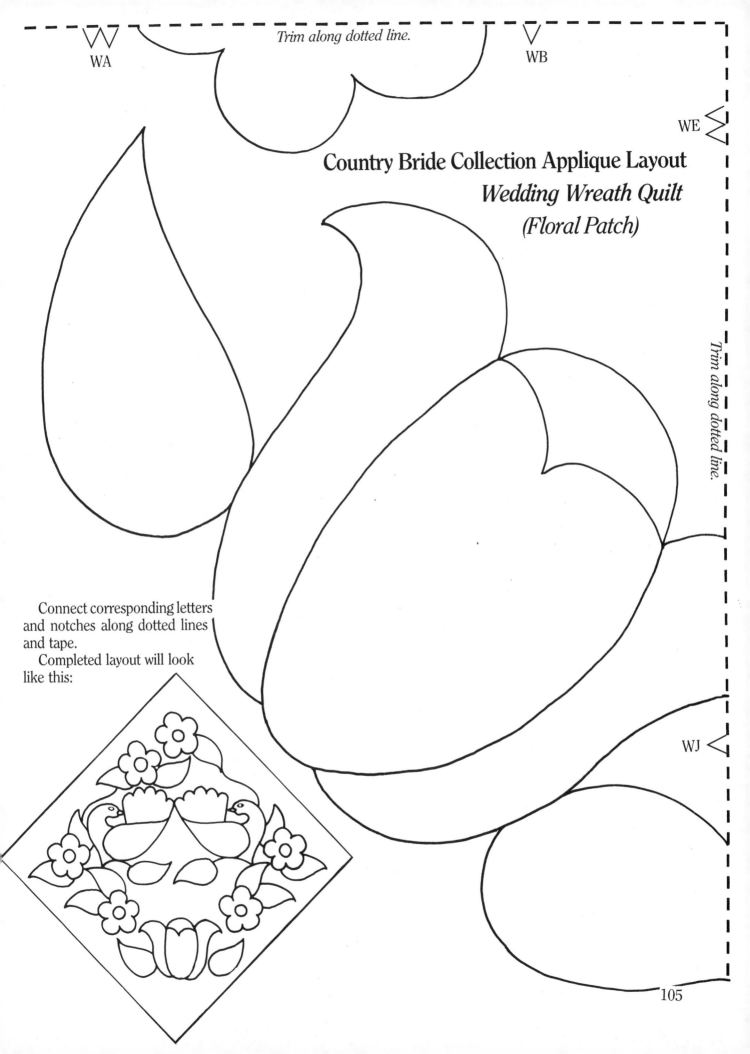

WA

WB

WE

Country Bride Collection Applique Layout
Wedding Wreath Quilt
(Floral Patch)

Trim along dotted line.

Connect corresponding letters and notches along dotted lines and tape.

Completed layout will look like this:

WJ

105

WF

WE

WG

WH

WM

Country Bride Collection Applique Layout
Wedding Wreath Quilt
(Floral Patch)

WJ

WI

Country Bride Collection Applique Layout
Wedding Wreath Quilt
(Floral Patch)

WK

WL

WO

WP

Trim along dotted line.

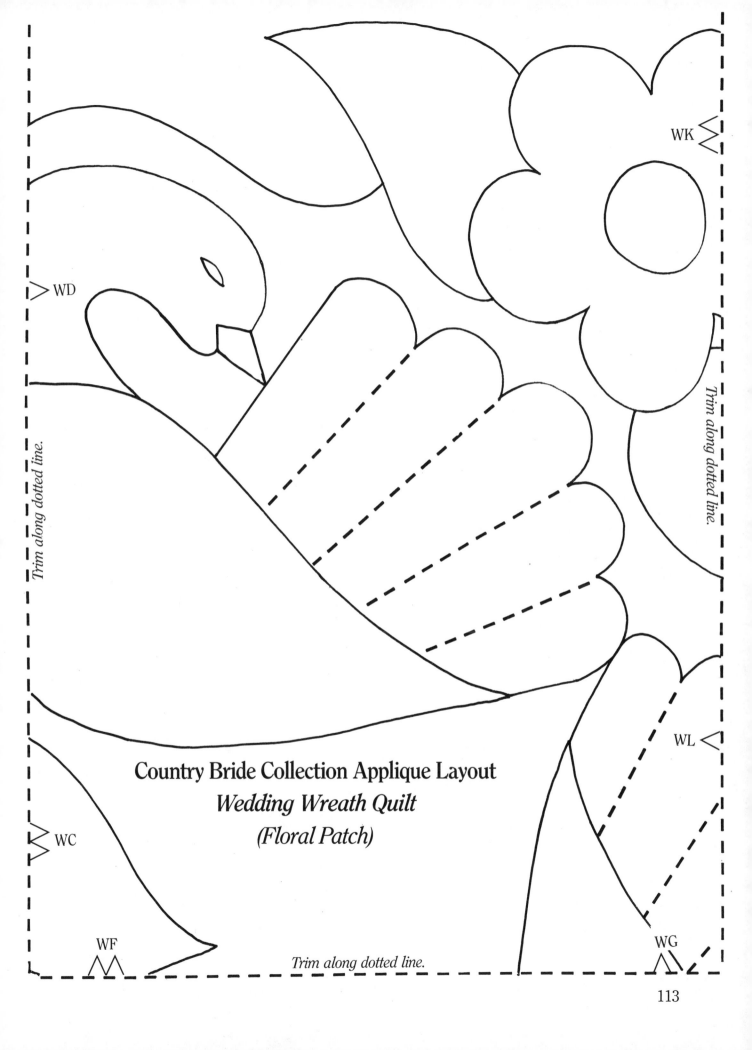

WD

WK

WL

Country Bride Collection Applique Layout
Wedding Wreath Quilt
(Floral Patch)

WC

WF

WG

Wedding Wreath Quilt
(Floral Patch)

WD

Trim along dotted line.

WC

WA

WB

Trim along dotted line.

Country Bride Collection Applique Layout
Country Wedding Wreath Quilt
(Small Triangle)

Connect corresponding letters
and notches along dotted lines
and tape.
    Completed layout will look
like this:

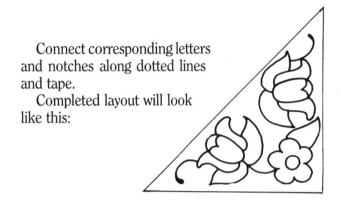

Trim along dotted line.

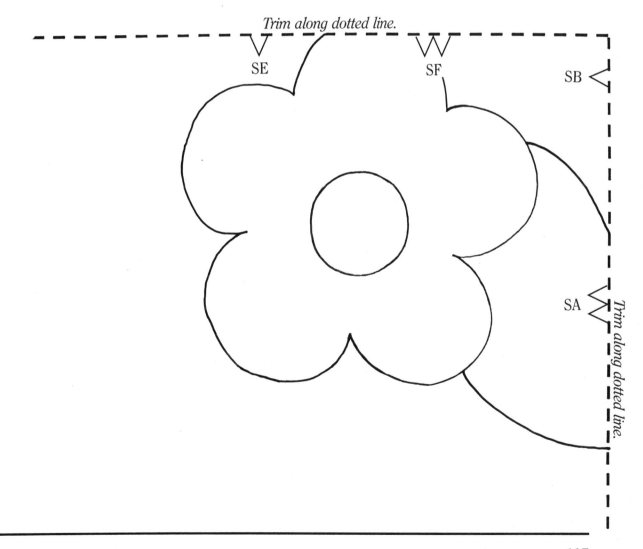

SE

SF

SB

SA

Trim along dotted line.

Country Bride Collection Applique Layout
Country Wedding Wreath Quilt
(Small Triangle)

Embroider or use narrow bias tape to create stems.

Trim along dotted line.

SD

SE

SF

SC

Trim along dotted line.

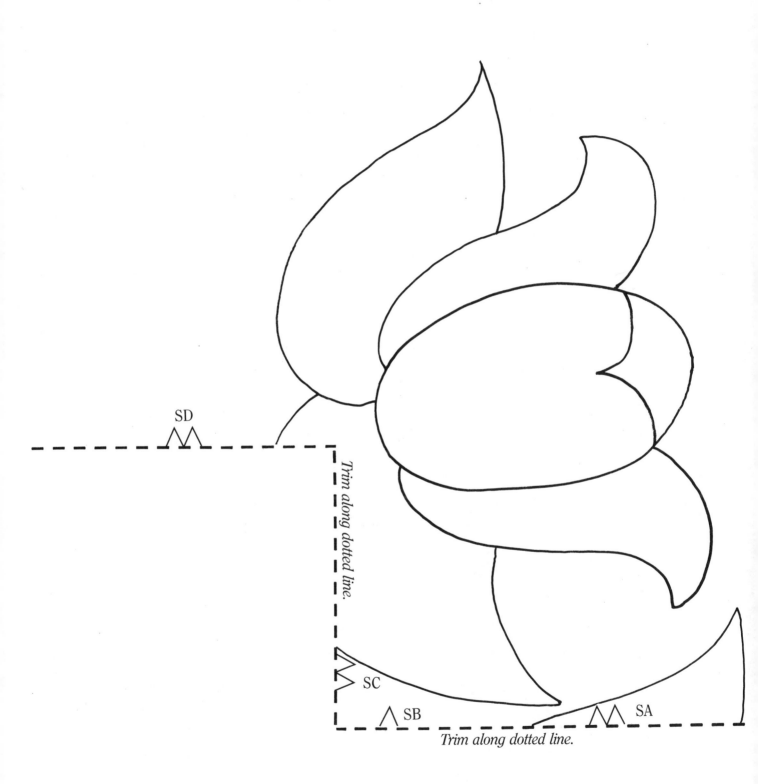

SD

Trim along dotted line.

SC

SB

SA

Trim along dotted line.

Country Bride Collection Applique Layout
Country Wedding Wreath Quilt
(Side Triangle)

Connect corresponding letters and notches along dotted lines and tape.
Completed layout will look like this:

Embroider or use narrow bias tape to create stems.

Trim along dotted line.

Trim along dotted line.

TD

TE

TB

TC

TF

TG

TA

TF

Trim along dotted line.

TB

TG

Trim along dotted line.

TC

Trim along dotted line.

TH

Country Wedding Wreath Quilt
(Side Triangle)

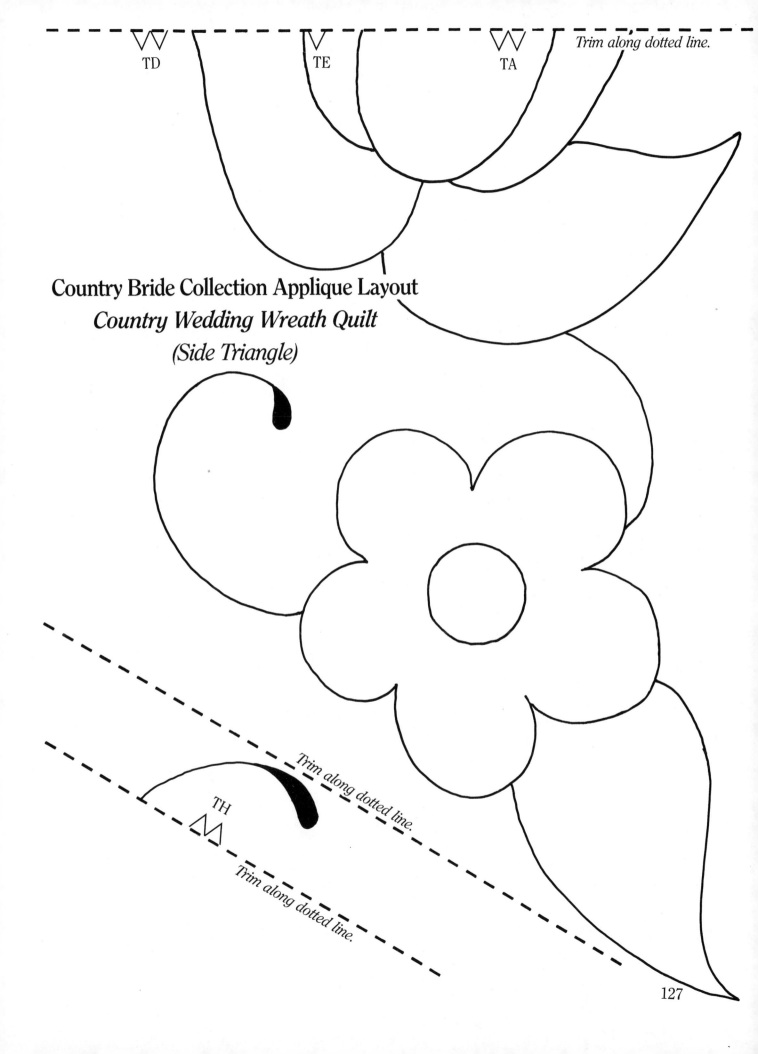

TD

TE

TA

Country Bride Collection Applique Layout
Country Wedding Wreath Quilt
(Side Triangle)

TH

Trim along dotted line.

Trim along dotted line.

127

Country Bride Collection Applique Layout
Country Wedding Wreath Quilt
(Wreath Patch)

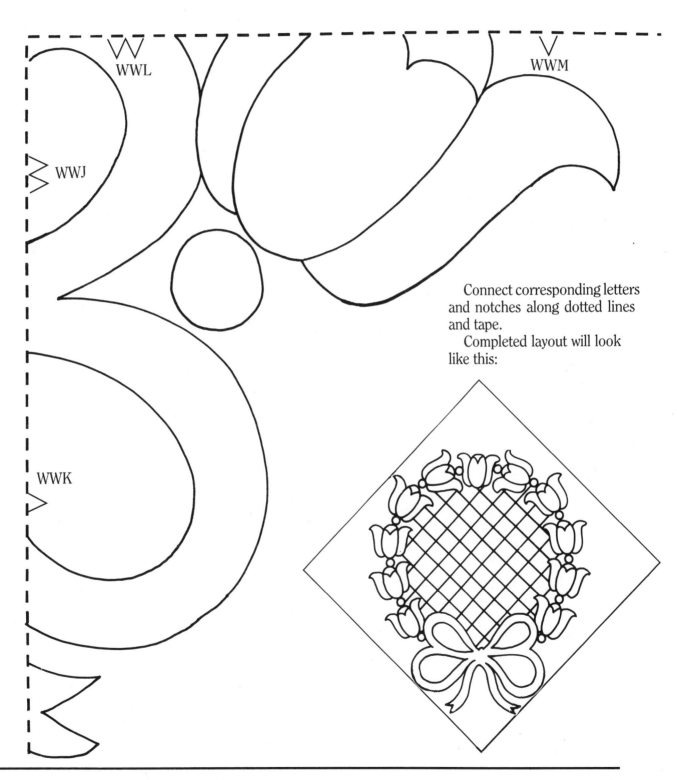

WWL

WWM

WWJ

Connect corresponding letters
and notches along dotted lines
and tape.

Completed layout will look
like this:

WWK

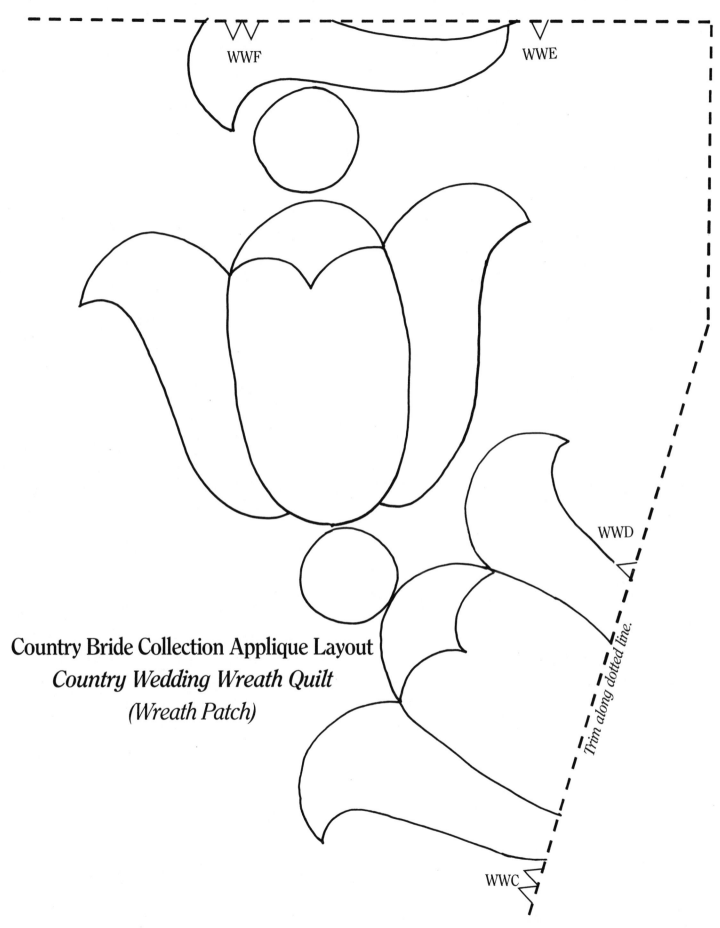

WWF

WWE

WWD

Trim along dotted line.

Country Bride Collection Applique Layout
Country Wedding Wreath Quilt
(Wreath Patch)

WWC

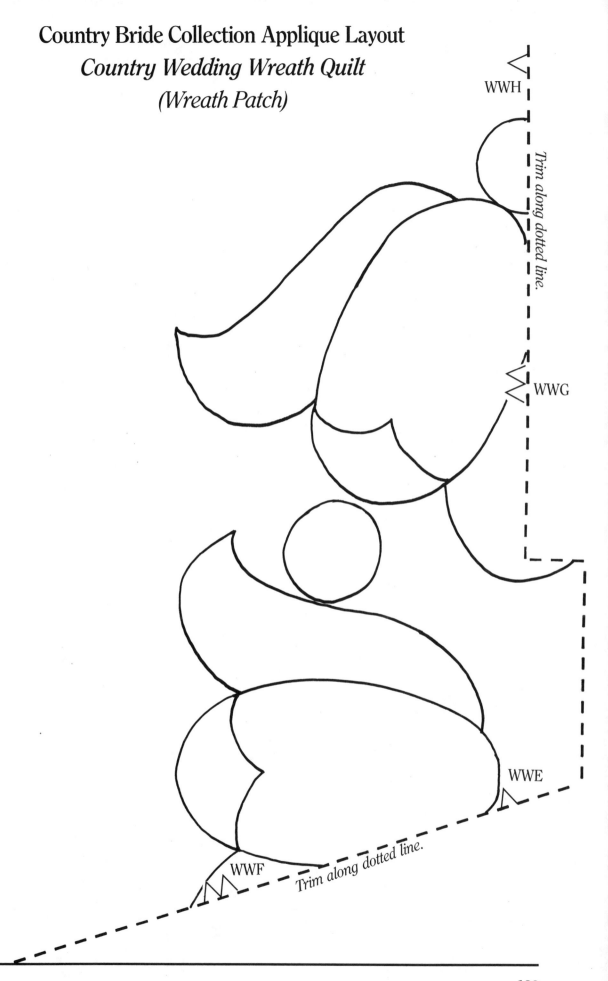

WWH

Trim along dotted line.

WWG

WWE

WWF

Trim along dotted line.

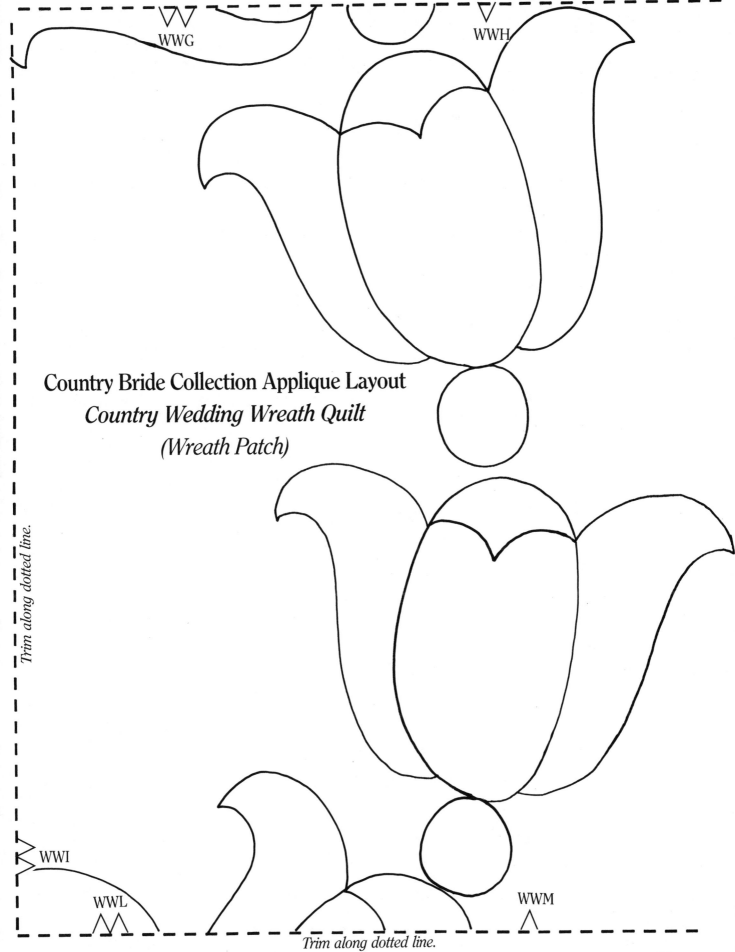

Country Bride Collection Applique Layout
Country Wedding Wreath Quilt
(Wreath Patch)

WWG

WWH

WWI

WWL

WWM

Trim along dotted line.

Trim along dotted line.

135

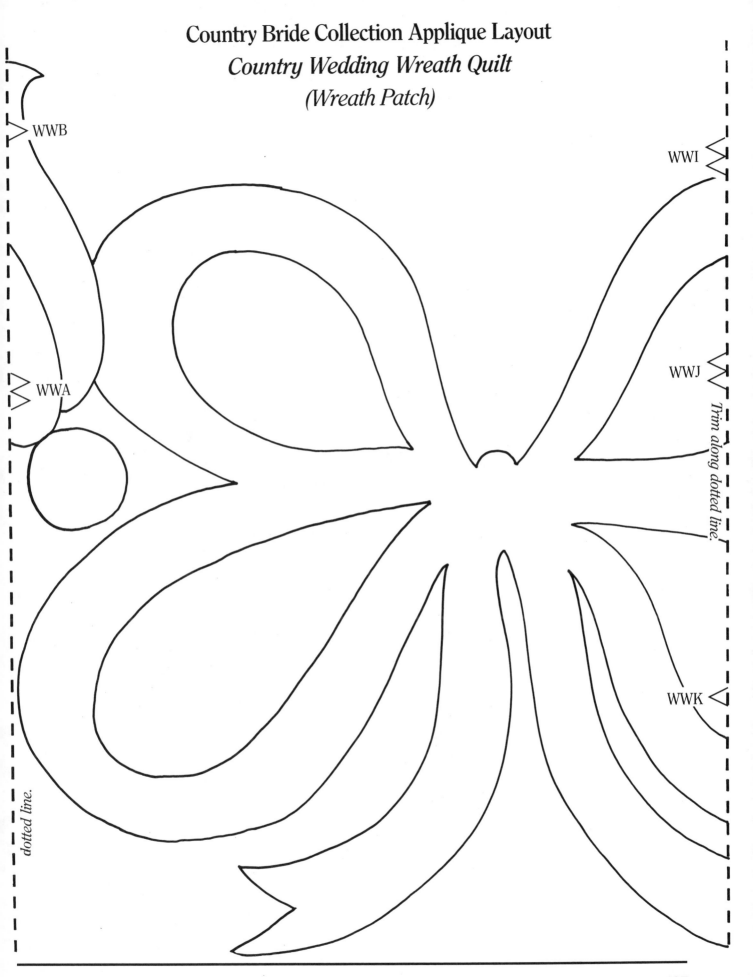

WWB

WWI

WWA

WWJ

Trim along dotted line.

dotted line.

WWK

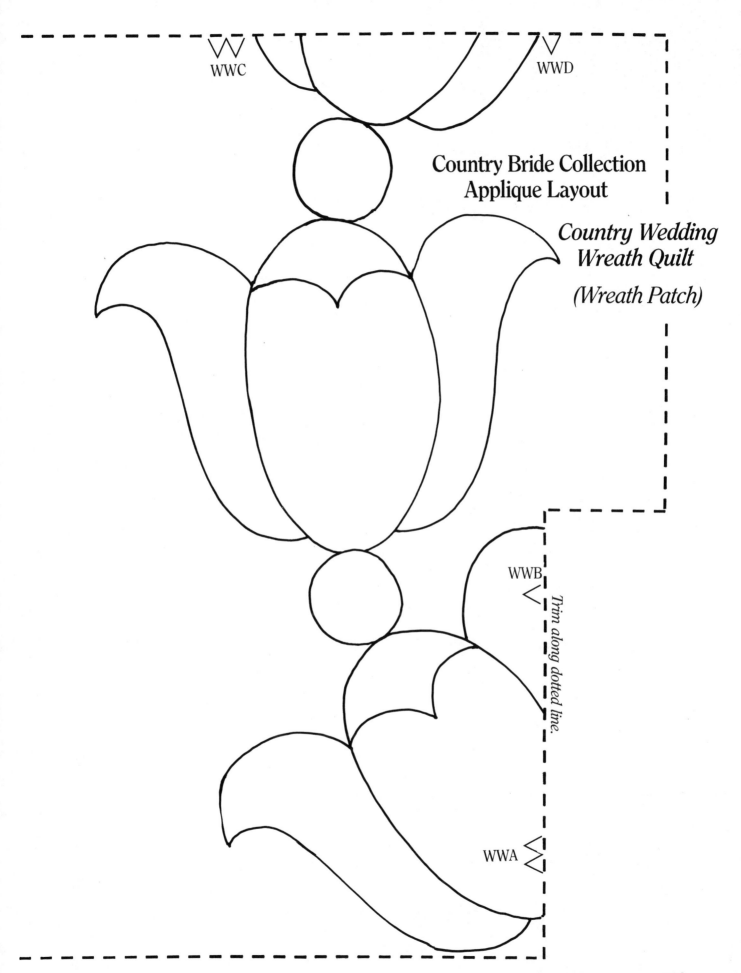

WWC

WWD

Country Bride Collection
Applique Layout

*Country Wedding
Wreath Quilt*

(Wreath Patch)

WWB

Trim along dotted line.

WWA

Country Bride Collection Applique Layout
Pillow Throw
(Same Layout for all the Quilts.)

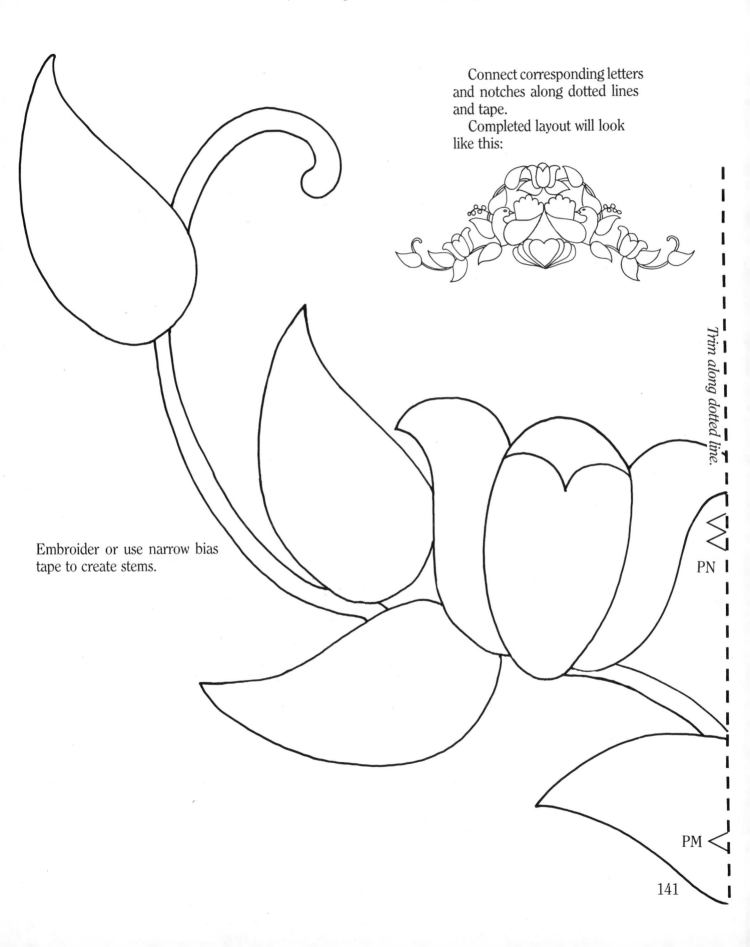

Connect corresponding letters
and notches along dotted lines
and tape.
    Completed layout will look
like this:

Embroider or use narrow bias
tape to create stems.

Trim along dotted line.

PN

PM

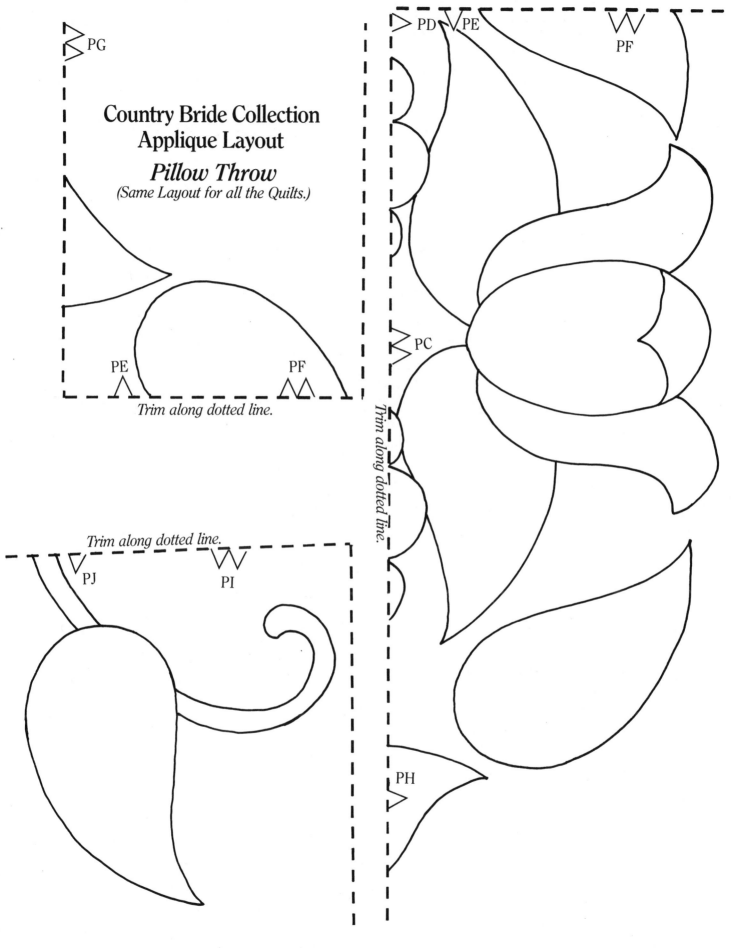

PG

Country Bride Collection
Applique Layout
Pillow Throw
(Same Layout for all the Quilts.)

PE   PF

Trim along dotted line.

Trim along dotted line.

PJ   PI

PD   PE   PF

PC

PH

Trim along dotted line.

143

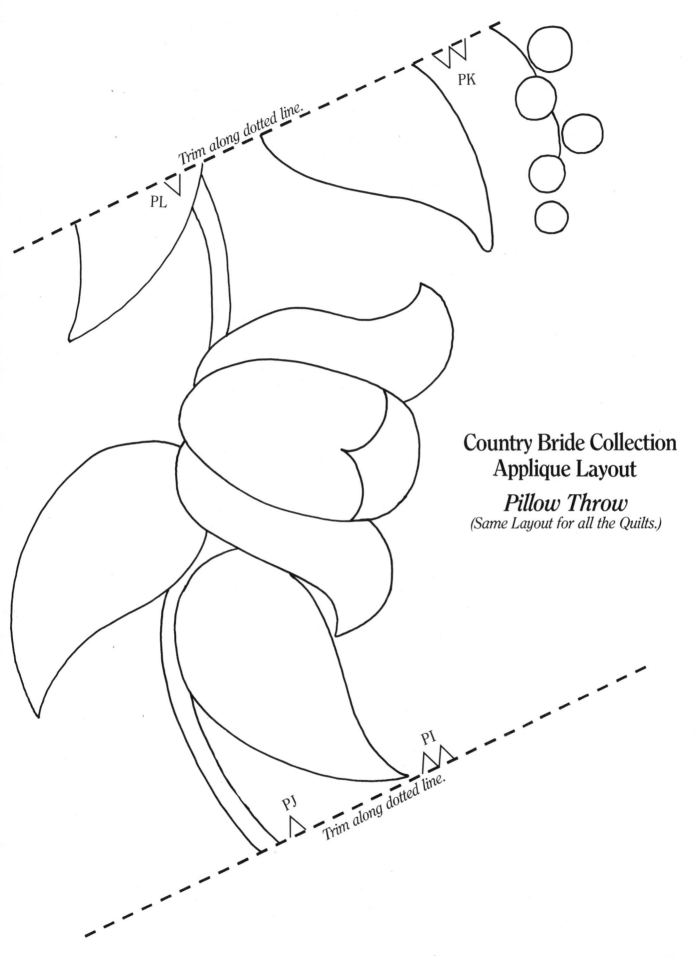

Trim along dotted line.

PL

PK

**Country Bride Collection
Applique Layout**

Pillow Throw
(Same Layout for all the Quilts.)

PI

PJ

Trim along dotted line.

Country Bride Collection Applique Layout
Pillow Throw
(Same Layout for all the Quilts.)

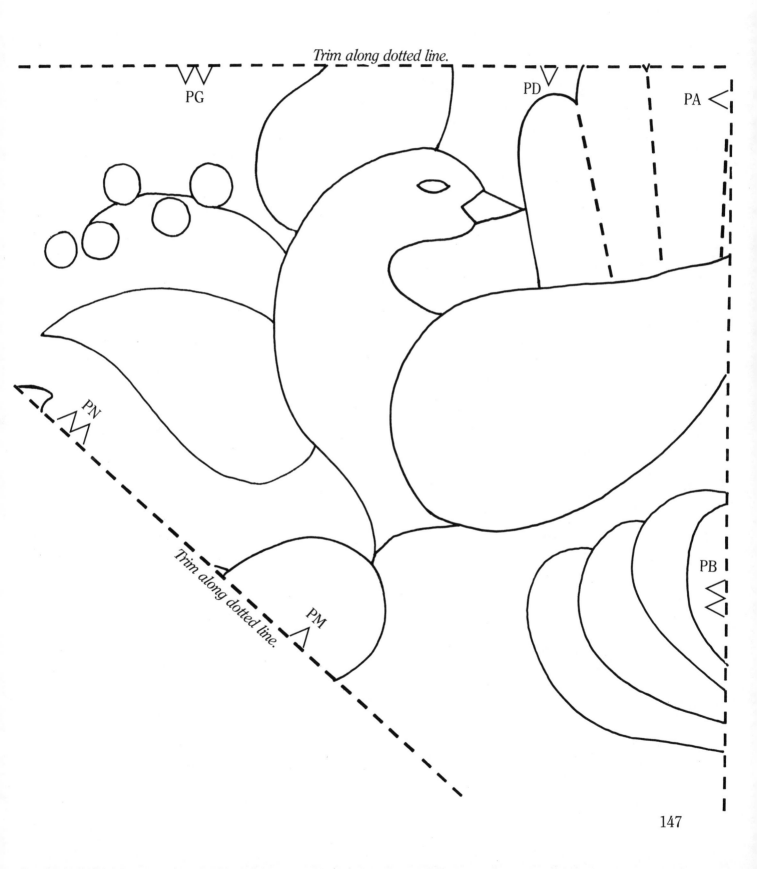

Trim along dotted line.

PG

PD

PA

PN

Trim along dotted line.

PM

PB

Country Bride Collection Applique Layout
Pillow Throw
(Same Layout for all the Quilts.)

Trim along dotted line.

PA

PC

PH

Trim along dotted line.

PK

PB

PL

Country Bride Collection Applique Layout
Country Courtship Quilt

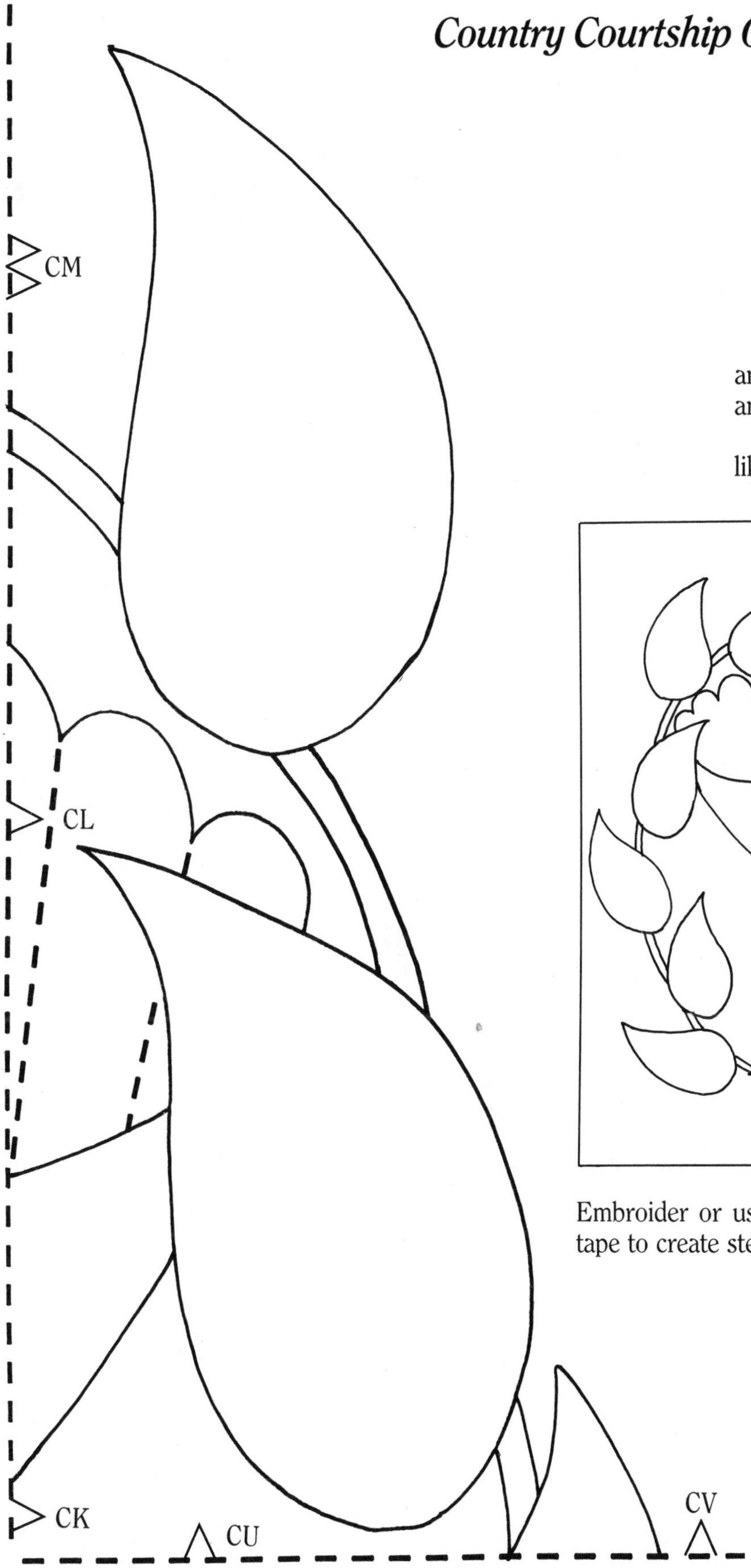

CM

CL

CK   CU   CV

Trim along dotted line.

Connect corresponding letters
and notches along dotted lines
and tape.
Completed layout will look
like this:

Embroider or use narrow bias
tape to create stems.

CG

CM

Trim along dotted line.

CL

CF

Trim along dotted line.

CH

CI

CJ

Trim along dotted line.

Country Bride Collection Applique Layout
Country Courtship Quilt

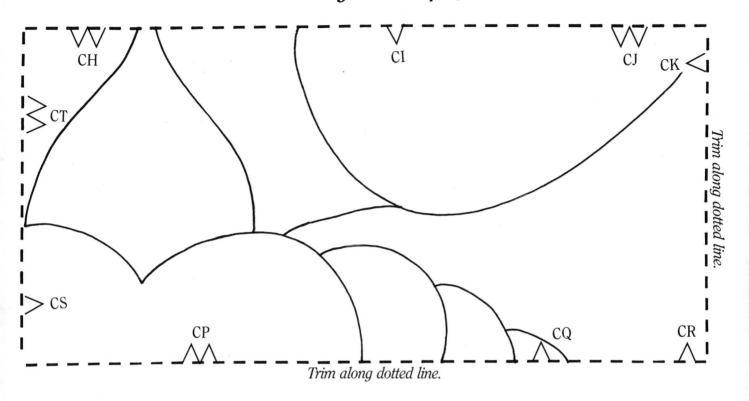

CH

CI

CJ

CK

CT

Trim along dotted line.

CS

CP

CQ

CR

Trim along dotted line.

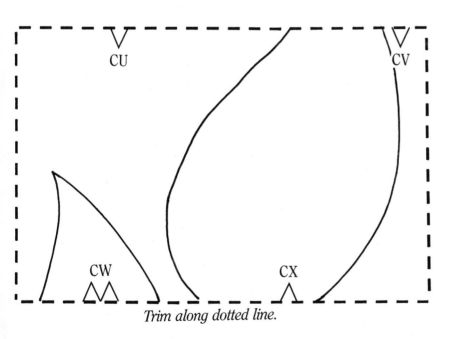

CU

CV

CW

CX

Trim along dotted line.

CG

Trim along dotted line.

CF

CA

CB

CC

Trim along dotted line.

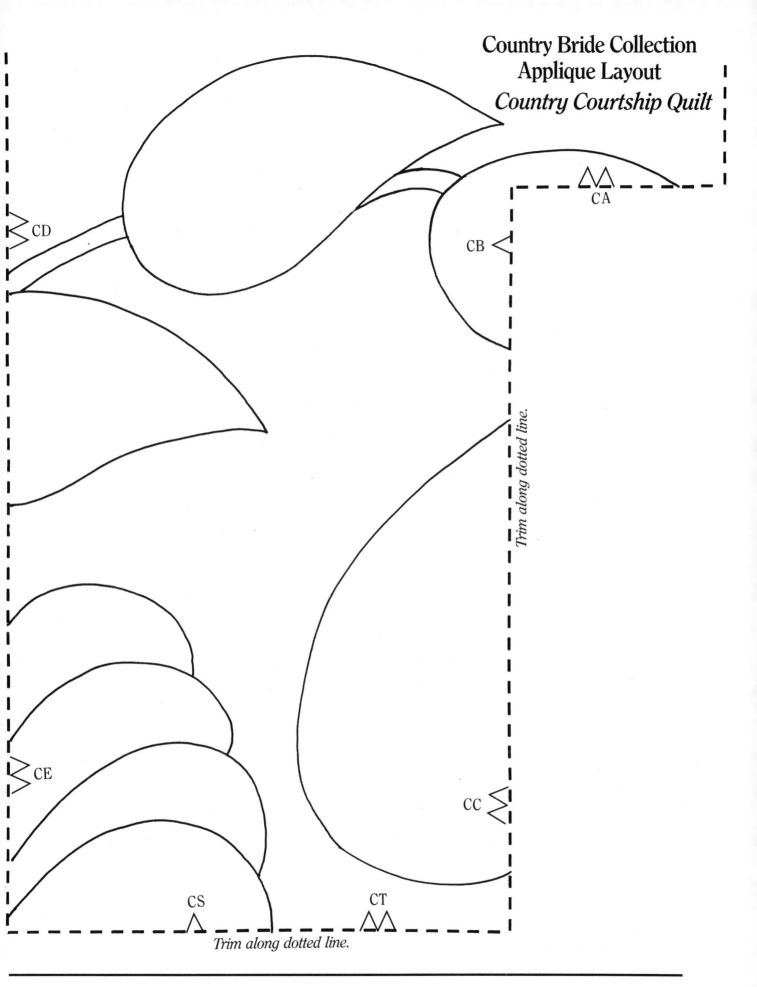

Country Bride Collection
Applique Layout
Country Courtship Quilt

CA

CD

CB

Trim along dotted line.

CE

CC

CS

CT

Trim along dotted line.

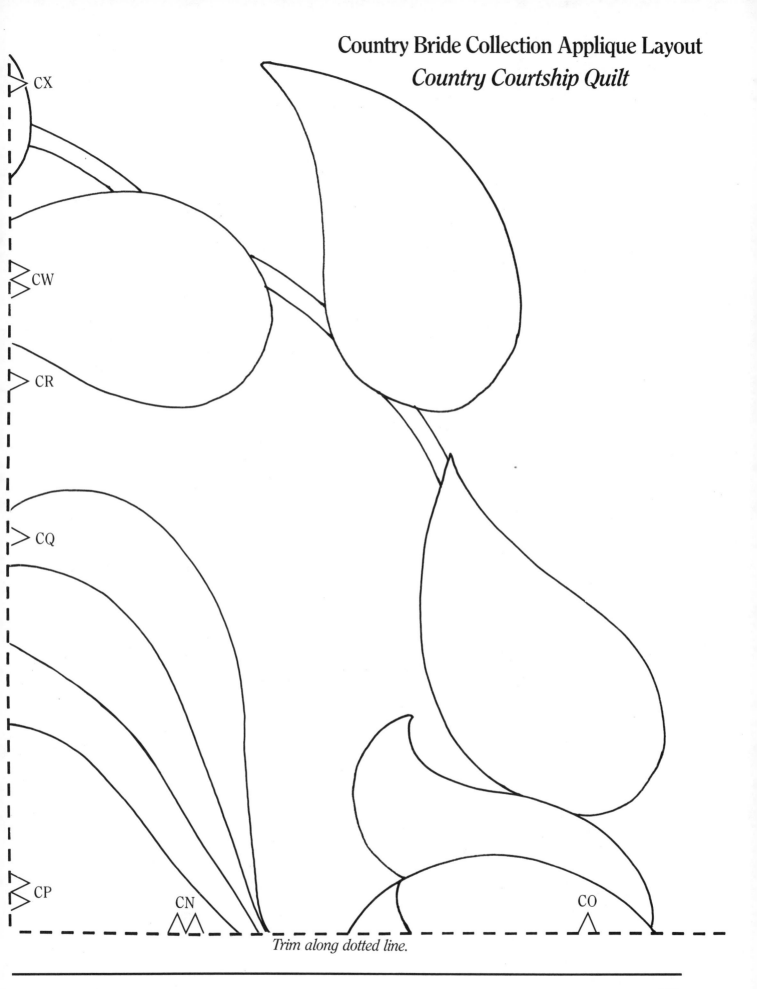

CX

CW

CR

CQ

CP

CN

CO

Trim along dotted line.

Country Bride Collection Applique Layout
Country Courtship Quilt

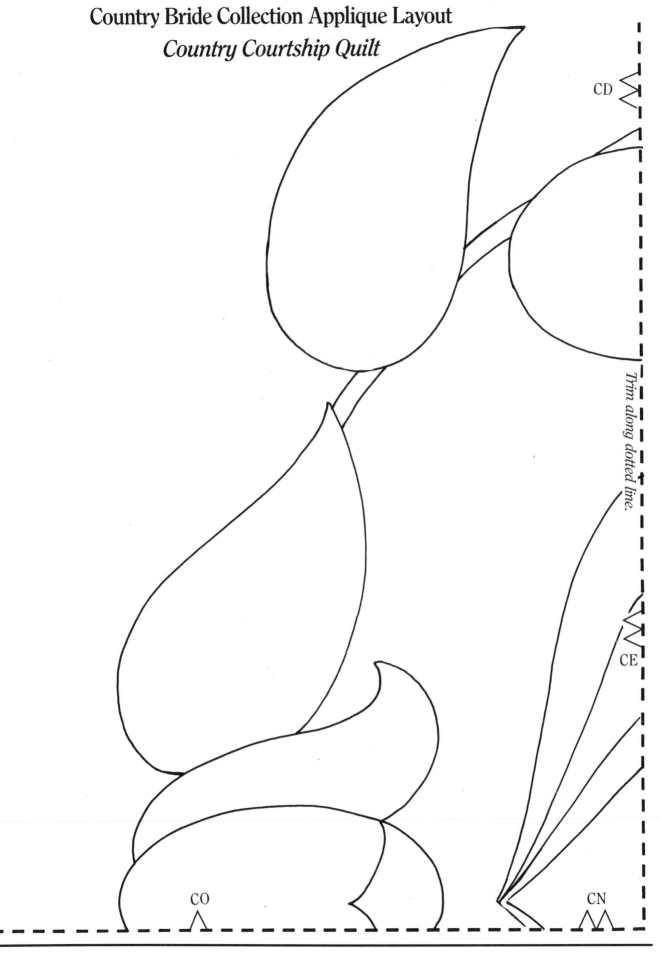

CD

Trim along dotted line.

CE

CO

CN

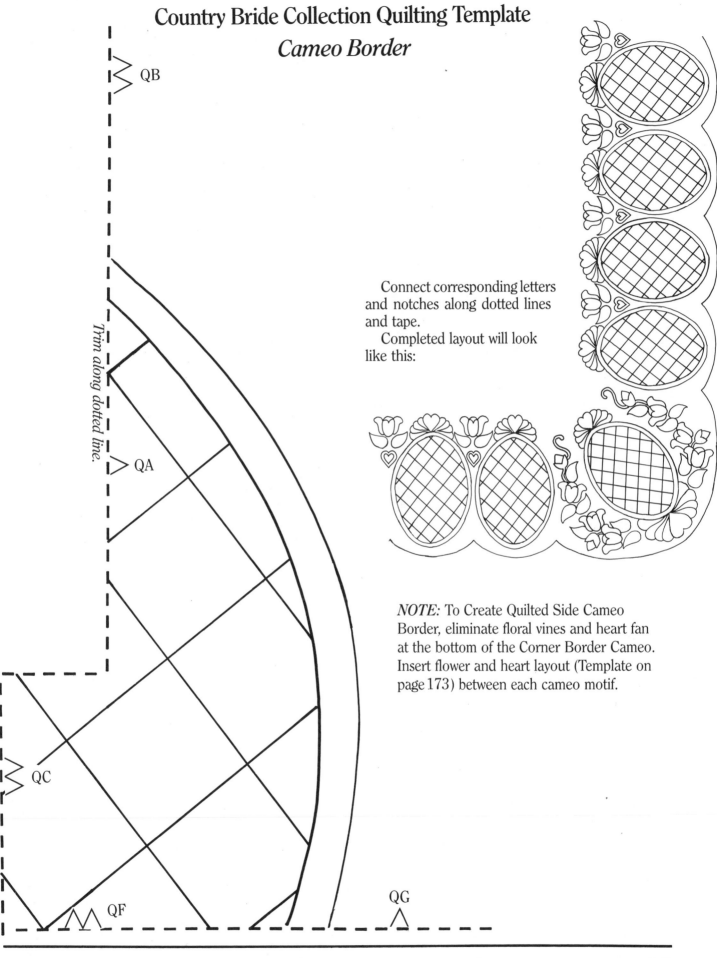

Country Bride Collection Quilting Template
Cameo Border

QB

Trim along dotted line.

QA

Connect corresponding letters and notches along dotted lines and tape.

Completed layout will look like this:

NOTE: To Create Quilted Side Cameo Border, eliminate floral vines and heart fan at the bottom of the Corner Border Cameo. Insert flower and heart layout (Template on page 173) between each cameo motif.

QC

QF

QG

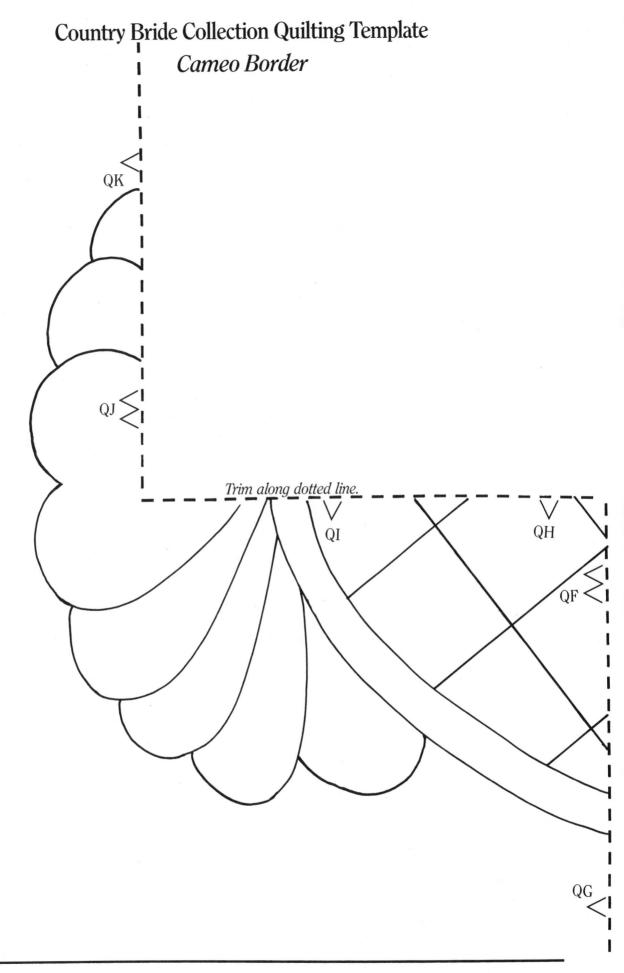

QK

QJ

Trim along dotted line.

QI

QH

QF

QG

W
QB

V QA

V
QD

Trim along dotted line.

QE **W**

Country Bride Collection
Quilting Template

Cameo Border

Flop this floral vine motif on the other
side of the cameo to create the entire
Corner Border.

169

Country Bride Collection
Quilting Template

Cameo Border

QE

Trim along dotted line.

QK

QJ

Trim along dotted line. QH

QC

QD

Country Bride Collection Quilting Template
Cameo Border

About The Old Country Store

The People's Place Quilt Museum

Cheryl A. Benner and Rachel T. Pellman are on the staff of The Old Country Store, located along Route 340 in Intercourse, Pennsylvania. The store offers crafts from more than 300 artisans, most of whom are local Amish and Mennonites. There are quilts of traditional and contemporary designs, patchwork pillows and pillow kits, afghans, stuffed animals, dolls, tablecloths and Christmas tree ornaments. Other handcrafted items include potholders, sunbonnets and wooden toys.

For the do-it-yourself quilter, the Store offers quilt supplies, fabric at discount prices, and a large selection of quilt books and patterns.

Located on the second floor of the Store is The People's Place Quilt Museum. The Museum, which opened in 1988, features antique Amish quilts and crib quilts as well as a small collection of dolls, doll quilts, socks and other decorative arts.

About the Authors

Cheryl A. Benner and Rachel T. Pellman together developed The Country Bride Collection designs. (Pellman is a co-author of the original Country Bride Quilt.) They created the patterns, then selected fabrics and supervised the making of the original quilts by Lancaster County Mennonite women. This is Benner's and Pellman's fourth collaboration on quilt designs with related books. Their earlier books are the popular *The Country Love Quilt, The Country Lily Quilt,* and *The Country Songbird Quilt.*

Benner, her husband Lamar, and young son live in Honeybrook, Pa. She is a graduate of the Art Institute of Philadelphia (Pa.). Benner is art director for Good Enterprises, Intercourse, Pa.

Pellman lives in Lancaster, Pa., and is manager of The Old Country Store, Intercourse. She is also the author of *Amish Quilt Patterns* and *Small Amish Quilt Patterns;* co-author with Jan Steffy of *Patterns for Making Amish Dolls and Doll Clothes;* and co-author with her husband, Kenneth, of *A Treasury of Amish Quilts, The World of Amish Quilts, Amish Crib Quilts,* and *Amish Doll Quilts, Dolls, and Other Playthings.*

The Pellmans are the parents of two sons.